# VICTORY IN SPIRITUAL WARFARE

## FIELD GUIDE FOR BATTLE

# TONY EVANS

B&H
PUBLISHING GROUP

Nashville, Tennessee

Published by B&H Publishing Group
© 2011 Tony Evans • Reprinted November 2020

ISBN 978-1-4300-5357-6

Dewey decimal classification: 235.4
Subject headings: SPIRITUAL WARFARE \ DEMONOLOGY \
BIBLE. N.T. EPHESIANS—STUDY

*Printed in the United States of America*

Groups Ministry Publishing • B&H Publishing Group
One LifeWay Plaza • Nashville, TN 37234

# CONTENTS

# ABOUT THE AUTHOR

*Dr. Tony Evans*

**Dr. Tony Evans** is one of America's most respected leaders in evangelical circles. He's a pastor, a best-selling author, and a frequent speaker at Bible conferences and seminars throughout the nation. He has served as the senior pastor of Oak Cliff Bible Fellowship for more than forty years, witnessing its growth from ten people in 1976 to more than ten thousand congregants with more than one hundred ministries.

Dr. Evans also serves as the president of The Urban Alternative, a national ministry that seeks to restore hope and transform lives through the proclamation and application of God's Word. His daily radio broadcast, *The Alternative with Dr. Tony Evans,* can be heard on more than 1,300 radio outlets throughout the United States and in more than 130 countries.

Dr. Evans holds the honor of writing and publishing the first full-Bible commentary and study Bible by an African-American. A former chaplain for the Dallas Cowboys, he's currently the chaplain for the NBA's Dallas Mavericks, a team he has served for more than thirty years.

Through his local church and national ministry, Dr. Evans has set in motion a kingdom-agenda philosophy of ministry that teaches God's comprehensive rule over every area of life, as demonstrated through the individual, family, church, and society.

Dr. Evans is married to Lois, his wife and ministry partner of more than forty years. They are the proud parents of four—Chrystal, Priscilla, Anthony Jr., and Jonathan—and have a number of grandchildren.

# GET IN THE FIGHT!

Whether you recognize it or not, there is currently a war going on all around you. It's a cosmic conflict of such ferocity, size, and scope that it makes all other wars pale in comparison. This is the battle being waged in the heavenlies, and it's a battle God is calling you to wake up to.

This wake-up call is being issued to Christian men and women, for the vast majority of us, though we know Christ and might have a pew reserved in church every Sunday, are nonetheless living defeated lives. We try and fail, and then try and fail again. No matter what we do, we can't seem to live in the way the Bible describes the life of the Christian.

## *We are plagued by anxiety, hang-ups, compulsions, and addictions.*
## No more!

God has already given the Christian everything needed to live in victory. Because of the life, death, and resurrection of Jesus Christ, victory is not only possible—it's already been assured. His victory is our victory. All that's left is for us to connect the visible, physical world with the victory already given to us in the invisible, spiritual world. Amazingly, we aren't fighting *for* victory; we are fighting *from* victory.

That's what this study is about—understanding and implementing the victory of Christ through the essential pieces of spiritual armor God has given the believer to wear.

Over the next eight sessions, we will learn about all God has already secured for the believer in Christ. We will discover together what each piece of armor is and how to put it on. We will see that this armor is to be employed every day in real life situations. And together, we will learn to live in the victory God has won for us in Christ.

# HERE'S HOW IT WORKS

This study includes opportunities for both individual and group study. Engaging in the individual daily devotions and then participating in a Bible study group, which includes video teaching and discussion, is the best way to gain the fullest understanding of *Victory in Spiritual Warfare*.

At the beginning of each session, you will find the guide for the Bible study group portion of the study. Each meeting should follow this general outline:

**Getting Started:** Each week will begin with a brief time of discussion that helps you and your group get to know each other better and discuss what the Lord has been teaching you over the previous week (10 min.).

**Arming Up:** Your group will watch a 30-40 minute teaching segment from the DVD while filling in the listening guide provided in this field guide. After the teaching segment, your group will briefly discuss the truths you've seen presented using the questions provided in the group experience. Then you will close with prayer.

**Get in the Fight:** The group experience each week wraps up with a key verse of Scripture to memorize and some specific challenges to engage in as you learn more about the tools God has given you for victory.

The teaching segment and discussion will propel you forward, as an individual, into your study throughout the week. Each day, you'll continue looking at the Scriptures and ideas presented in your group by completing the five personal devotions. The next week, you will come back to your group ready to begin another discussion based on the individual work you've done.

Throughout these eight sessions, you'll begin to see life as you never have before. You will sense the magnitude of the battle around you, and begin to see the power available to the Christian who is willing to grab onto it. I pray that God will show you the measure of victory He has already assured you.

# NOW LET'S GET IN THE FIGHT!

# SESSION 1

THE WAR REVEALED

# SESSION 1 | THE WAR REVEALED

## GETTING STARTED

1. Introduce yourself, and share one personal fact that will help your group get to know you better.

2. Share what you hope to gain from this study.

3. How familiar would you say that you are with the subject of spiritual warfare?

## ARMING UP

**Watch the teaching segment from the DVD using the viewer guide below.**

The whole Old Testament is a "move-countermove" battle between _____ and _____.

Satan's final move was the crucifixion and _____ of Jesus Christ.

God's final move was the _____ of Jesus Christ.

No matter what your circumstances, the accomplishment of the cross and resurrection of Jesus is your final move for _____.

The battles we have in life are not fundamentally _____ in nature.

Whatever is, has, or will go on in your life is rooted first in the _____ realm.

Spiritual warfare is the conflict in the _____ realm that affects the visible realm. It is the battle in the unseen that is responsible for the battles in the _____.

_____ you will ever need has already been deposited in your account in the unseen realm.

The demonic realm knows your _____.

The _____ world manifests what is happening in the spiritual world.

In order to fix what is manifested in the physical, you must go back to its origin in the _____.

If all you _____ is what you see, then you do not see all there is to be seen.

If you want to fix the _____ and physical, you must address the _____ and spiritual.

Satan's one overarching strategy is to _____.

The only power Satan and demons have is the power _____ give them.

The Devil operates by _____ and _____.

"Stand firm" means stay in the area where _____ has already been achieved.

**Discuss the teaching with your group, using the questions below.**

1. How might your perspective on your own struggles begin to change if you focused on their spiritual origins?

2. Why is it important to know that you are fighting from victory, rather than fighting for victory?

3. How might you better prepare yourself for spiritual attack that will come against you this week?

**Close with prayer.**

Video sessions available at www.bhpublishinggroup.com/victoryinspiritualwarfare
or with a subscription to smallgroup.com

# GET IN THE FIGHT!

"Our battle is not against flesh and blood, but against the authorities, against the world powers of this darkness, against the spiritual forces of evil in the heavens." Ephesians 6:12

- This week, as you come into difficulty, ask God to open your eyes to the spiritual reality behind the physical experience.

- Pray for spiritual awareness and sensitivity to recognize the subtle attacks of the Evil One.

# SESSION ONE

In the blockbuster film *Inception* the main characters discovered a way to enter another realm—the realm of dreams. Though the dream seemed as vivid and authentic as the real world, the dream realm was not their reality.

Because the dream felt real to their five senses, each character created an item used to let others know if they were in a dream or in reality. Without the item, the person in the dream might believe the dream was reality, and they might stay there—operating by the laws of reality within the realm of the dream.

The main character's item was a spinning top. If his top kept spinning endlessly, that meant he was in a dream. If it fell, he had woken up. The knowledge that he was in a dream enabled him to take more risks and live differently because he knew at any time, he could simply wake up in reality.

Is it possible that right now our ultimate reality isn't happening in the physical world as we see it? Could it be that right now there is a spiritual battle waging all around us in the unseen realms and that battle has physical effects in this world? If that's true, then most of us walk around in this world with no idea of what's happening in the spiritual one. The top keeps on spinning.

The spiritual world is real. Conversations, decisions, and battles that occur in the spiritual realm unilaterally impact what takes place in our physical lives. Unless we realize that truth and wake up to the battle, we will continue to look for physical solutions to solve spiritual problems manifesting themselves in our physical lives.

*Time to wake up and get in the real fight.*

# DAY 1 | WHAT IS SPIRITUAL WARFARE?

We are engaged in war. In fact, this war is like no other war that we have ever known, heard about, or could even conceive. Its implications reach further and its casualties devastate more than any conflict in the history of humankind. Strangely, though, most people walk around completely unaware that it's taking place.

What about you? On the scale below, mark your awareness of spiritual warfare.

_____

Unaware                                                        Very aware

What makes spiritual warfare different from other conflicts in the world?

What are the dangers of being unaware of this ongoing battle?

Above and beyond its sheer magnitude and scope, a major difference between this war and other wars is that this war is fought in a place we have never seen. *Spiritual warfare* can be defined as *the cosmic conflict waged in the invisible, spiritual realm that is simultaneously fleshed out in the context of the visible, physical realm.* To put it another way, you can't see the root of the war, but you can certainly see—and feel—the effects.

In fact, there is a spiritual root behind every physical disturbance, setback, ailment, or issue we face.

Look at the previous definition of *spiritual warfare*. Have you ever felt directly engaged in the invisible realm?

How about the physical? What is one instance when you think you've clearly felt or seen the physical effects of the battle?

Too often we restrict our battles to physical. We battle the physical temptation to sin, the physical injustice prevalent in impoverished nations, and the physical evil of persecuting governments, to name a few. But if we restrict our focus to the physical realm, victory will be only temporary and shallow. It's a little like putting a bandage on a wound when there is internal hemorrhaging.

If we really want to get in the fight, we must equip ourselves with the armor of God, which allows us to fight not just the effects of the war but the root of the conflict. To do that, we must understand who, what, and where we are fighting.

Read Ephesians 6:10-12. According to Paul, whom is our battle *not* against?

Who are our opponents?

Where does the battle take place?

Our battle is not against our neighbor, spouse, coworker, child, or even our own propensities and weaknesses in our flesh. People are simply a conduit for the spiritual battle taking place in another realm—the heavens. The "heavens" (v. 12) simply means *in the spiritual realm*.

That's a hard truth to grasp because it's easier to do battle with the physical. We feel wronged in some way, and we want someone or something physical at which to lash out. But doing that is like a police officer watching TV in his living room and pulling a gun on a criminal he sees on a reality TV show. If the officer shoots at the television, he will merely add more mess to the mess that is already going on. It might make him feel better for a moment that he did something, but in the end nothing has been solved. In fact, things have only gotten worse.

Whatever has gone on, is going on, or will go on in your visible, physical world is rooted in the invisible, spiritual realm. If you do not know how to navigate in the spiritual realm, you can't hope to truly fix anything in this one.

Let that last paragraph sink in. Does that mean there is no place for action in the physical world? Why or why not?

Describe the kind of perspective you would need to do battle in the spiritual realm in order to effect physical change.

When you're active in the spiritual battle, it doesn't mean you won't have tough conversations with coworkers and family. Nor does it mean you spend all your time hiding in your closet praying. Far from it. When actively engaged in the spiritual realm, you can move with confidence and power in the physical one because you're prepared and ready.

You're no longer content to settle for easy fixes and minor wins. You've tapped into the secret to abundant life and spiritual victory. You're living—and fighting—at a deeper level than most people.

But you've also come to realize that the opponents you face are more dangerous, treacherous, and numerous than you ever thought possible.

Pray today that God will begin to sharpen your spiritual sense so that you can begin to see the true nature of the battles before you.

## DAY 2 | THE ENEMY

Most of us, if we even believe Satan exists, think we'd easily recognize him. He's the guy with the red suit and horns, right? Not quite. That's too obvious. His scheme is to trick you. He doesn't want you to see him for who he truly is. He's not merely hanging out at the First Church of Hell. Rather, he's concerned with finding a way to infiltrate First Baptist, First Methodist, or First Bible Church of Anytown, USA.

In fact, Satan is very content that most people don't believe he exists. Why? Because if you don't take the spiritual realm seriously, there's no chance you can ever find spiritual victory in this life. Maybe the greatest trick the Devil ever pulled was convincing the world he doesn't exist.

What three words come to mind when you think of Satan?

1.

2.

3.

Why is it important to be informed about Satan?

Read Isaiah 14:12-15. According to this passage, what was Lucifer's great sin?

According to the Bible, the spiritual battle began when God created the angels. Lucifer, the anointed angel, became proud of his great beauty and rebelled against God, taking one third of the angels with him. From that moment on, the battle in the heavens has raged on.

The first time we see Satan in Scripture, he's slithering around in the form of a snake in the garden of Eden.

Read Genesis 3:1. How does the Bible describe Satan in this passage?

Why is the serpent a fitting form for him to take in light of this description?

The reason Satan took on the form of a snake is because he, along with his demons, operates best when there is a physical presence through which to work. Though spiritual warfare is being waged in heavenly places, our Enemy is very skilled at locating available vehicles in the physical realm through which to influence, manipulate, and deceive.

This particular physical form fits the character of the Enemy. A snake creeps and slithers. He slips into dark, unexpected places. A snake strikes without warning. That's the way the Enemy works—not overt but covert. Not obvious but subtle.

Paul shows us a clip of Satan's major game plan in Ephesians 6:10-11: "Be strengthened by the Lord and by His vast strength. Put on the full armor of God so that you can stand against the tactics of the Devil." The word *tactics* simply means *deceptive strategies*. Satan's overarching strategy, which he carries out in many ways, is to deceive. He is the ultimate magician operating not only with smoke and mirrors but also by sleight of hand.

Read 2 Corinthians 11:14. How does this verse relate to Ephesians 6:10-11?

Do you think you take the deceptive strategies of Satan seriously enough? Why or why not?

If Satan is the master of deception, how do you think you can more effectively recognize his tricks?

Genesis 3 is a case study in this kind of trickery. If Satan had been interested in a frontal, direct assault, he might have sought to do physical harm to the humans in the garden. Or he could have argued with them that God was evil or didn't exist at all. But he went with a far more devious—and ultimately more effective—form of attack.

Read Genesis 3:1-6. Describe Satan's tactic in these verses.

Why do you think this methodology was more successful than a frontal, direct assault?

One of the Devil's main tricks is to cause you to miss the goodness of God. As he did with Eve in the garden, Satan wants you to question the value of all the trees that God provided by getting you to focus on the one tree God said to avoid. It's just a small seed of doubt and discontent, but that seed grows and grows in our hearts.

I wonder when Eve recognized that the snake was really the Devil in disguise. When she talked herself into tasting the fruit? As she took the bite? When Adam did? Probably not. She probably wasn't aware that an attack was under way until the attack was already over and the battle won.

Can you think of a specific instance when you realized too late that you were under spiritual attack?

What might you have done to be more on guard against the attack in the first place?

Satan is on the attack. Just because we don't see him doesn't mean he's not there, plotting against us all.

Pray today that you will begin to be wary of spiritual attacks from places you would least expect.

# DAY 3  THE ATTACK

Like any battle, spiritual warfare is filled with strategy from two sides—good and evil. Part of any good battle plan involves discovering the strategy of the other side. Once we know the strategy of the Enemy, we will be ready to counter his moves effectively. Satan's battle plan involves the overall tactic of deception and has four stages of warfare. The first stage begins with desire.

> Does the word *desire* have a positive or negative connotation? Why?

Desire isn't bad. Legitimate desire motivates us and provides an avenue for obtaining satisfaction and delight. But Satan takes a legitimate desire and corrupts it so that we satisfy that desire through illegitimate means.

> Can you think of a legitimate desire that is often fulfilled through illegitimate means?

A desire for food is good; gluttony is a sin. A desire for sex is good; immorality is a sin. A desire for sleep is good; laziness is a sin. Satan's initial strategy is to take a legitimate, God-given desire in our lives and twist it into something illegitimate. He knows the desire can't be avoided or ignored—God has planted it within us. So Satan tries to warp that desire by influencing how it is directed and used.

> Specifically, which of your legitimate desires does Satan most often corrupt? Why do you think he chooses that particular desire?

The second stage in Satan's strategy is the direct use of deception. Like a fisherman trying to catch a fish, Satan doesn't put his hook in the water all by itself. Instead, he puts a worm on the hook to deceive the fish—or person, into thinking they are getting something tasty.

Satan doesn't advertise the local club by saying, "Come here and get drunk, become addicted to drugs or alcohol, lose your family, and throw away your future." He starts with something small—just a single screenshot from the Internet, a conversation you shouldn't have had, or a relationship you shouldn't have made. But that's only the entry point. He tricks you into thinking you're getting something with no consequences.

> Read Numbers 1:1-2 and 1 Chronicles 21:1. David decided to take a census of the nation of Israel. Was taking a census, in and of itself, a sinful act?

> How do you see Satan using deception with David?

David succumbed to the temptation of pride. He was deceived into thinking a census was no big deal. However, David took a census because he was convinced his army was so large that he didn't need God, and as a result, 70 thousand people died. The point is that whatever controls our minds controls our actions.

The third stage in Satan's strategy is disobedience. Desire leads to deception, which then leads to disobedience.

> Read James 1:15. According to this passage, what does desire give birth to?

Desire is not sin. Sin is the illegitimate application and placement of desire. For example, when a young child makes a decision, it is often based on feelings and desires. The child first *feels* like playing, watching TV, or eating, and then carries out the action of playing, watching, or eating. But part of maturing is learning to manage those desires appropriately. The same thing must happen spiritually. Victorious Christian living occurs when the Holy Spirit's presence is free to manage our feelings, emotions, and desires.

In the progression in James, however, the Holy Spirit's presence is not free to manage. There is only desire that deeply roots itself and then is fulfilled in whatever way is most readily available.

In James 1:15 what does the progression eventually lead to?

In what ways have you seen "death" show up due to that progression in your own life?

That's the fourth stage. Sin produces death in a variety of ways, all bringing about the diminished ability to experience God's promise of the abundant life. This death can show up as the death of a dream, relationship, career, virtue, or any other number of areas. Primarily, though, sin produces a death within the fullness of our spirits as our fellowship is broken with God.

Satan is so effective at implementing this strategy from start to finish that he tries to work himself out of a job by training the deceived to become deceivers themselves. He turns people into "deception evangelists," spreading his lies quickly and effectively among us.

That's the strategy of the Enemy in this very real war. There are casualties all around us. But despite the strength and cunning of the Enemy, there is good news for us. Even though Satan's agenda and strategy are all-encompassing, they have already been defeated. But we must believe in the victory.

Pray that God will show you the areas of your life in which death is reigning. Express your trust in His ability to bring new life from death.

# DAY 4 | THE VICTORY

Satan may be the master of deception, but God is the master of reversal. Time after time throughout the history of the spiritual battle, Satan has put his best weapons and tactics forward. But time after time God has countered and brought good out of evil. The event that most clearly illustrates this reversal is the cross of Christ.

Consider the crucifixion of Jesus. How do you think Satan felt that day?

How should God's ability to dramatically reverse this apparent victory for Satan change the way you approach your own life circumstances?

The Son of God was brutally executed. Evil had won—or so it seemed. Three long days of silence from the heavens seemed to confirm that victory. But Satan miscalculated something very important. The cross was really the setup for God's ultimate victory over Satan by raising Jesus from the dead.

The accomplishment of the cross, through the resurrection of Christ, determined the ultimate outcome of the spiritual war. Because Jesus was raised from the dead, victory was secured. In light of His resurrection, each one of us can have victory over an Enemy who is seeking to intimidate, deceive, and destroy us.

What you and I need to do, while we are still on earth and the battles rage on, is to live in light of the ultimate victory. Because of the resurrection, Satan has no more authority over you. His only means to overcome and defeat you is through deception—making you believe the winner of the war is not yet decided.

*What specifically would be different about the way you thought about spiritual warfare if you believed the victory was already decided?*

Paul uses the word *heavens* a number of times in the Book of Ephesians, letting us know both the scope and occupants of the location of the spiritual battle. His first reference to this realm comes in chapter 1, when he writes, "Praise the God and Father of our Lord Jesus Christ, who has blessed us in Christ with every spiritual blessing in the heavens" (Eph. 1:3).

We learn from this verse that everything God is ever going to do for us He has already done. Every spiritual blessing is already located in this unseen realm. Every promise God has ever made and plans to fulfill on your behalf, every gift you will ever receive, and every hope that will ever be satisfied has already been deposited in your account in the spiritual realm. God has "blessed us in Christ with every spiritual blessing in the heavens." Your blessings and victory are already there with your name written on them, waiting for you to grab them, use them, and walk in them.

*What obstacles in your life keep you from fully believing Ephesians 1:3?*

*Do you think most Christians know and believe this verse? Why or why not?*

Many believers live defeated lives because they are unaware of this truth. In spiritual warfare, Satan tries to deceive you into believing that God is holding out on you and it's up to you to get God to give you both blessings and victory. Satan wants you to think if you pray more, give more, serve more, or sin less, maybe God will give you more. This thinking shifts the focus from God and what He has already done in the spiritual realm and puts that focus on you and what you need to do in the physical realm. While doing those things in the physical realm is good, it is not the key to access what God has already given you in the spiritual realm.

Read Ephesians 6:10. According to this verse, what are we supposed to do?

From where does that strength come?

In grace God has made every believer complete in Jesus Christ. Grace—not works—is the point of access to God. The way we enter this point of access is through faith. Faith is believing that God is telling the truth. The job of faith is to discover what the spiritual blessings in the heavenly places already are and to make life choices in that reality.

In the end it means we are called to firmly stand, not in our own strength but accessing the strength of God on our behalf. We do that not by trying harder but by believing harder in what He's already done in Christ.

When we do that, we find we are no longer fighting for victory but fighting from victory.

Reflect on that last statement. What difference would fighting from a stance of victory make in a spiritual battle?

For the rest of our study together, we'll discover those spiritual blessings God has already given to us. And we'll find out that believing in those blessings will not only help us stand but also help us armor up.

Pray today that you will have a growing understanding of the victory God has already won in Christ.

# THE ARMOR

We are fighting the spiritual battle, not for victory but from victory. God has already won the war in Christ. He's given us everything we need in Christ to see His victory lived out in every battle we enter. But that begs the question: If the war is already won and we have all we need for the individual battles, why don't more Christians experience spiritual victory?

On the scale below, rate the usual outcome of your spiritual battles:

_____

Frustration                                                                                      Victory

Why did you answer the way you did?

The Enemy is victorious in our lives because we yield the power to him by not standing firm in our identity in Jesus Christ. We fail to firmly remain in the union we were designed to have with Christ, under His headship.

Read Colossians 1:9-17. Summarize this passage in your own words with a few sentences.

Why do you think Paul chose to emphasize these truths about Jesus?

Jesus Christ holds all things together. Therefore, if you find yourself falling apart, it is a result of you not standing firm with Jesus in union with Him. Our union with Christ is essential to our victory over Satan's rule in our lives. We are *in Him* and *with Him.*

When Christ died, we died with Him. When Christ arose, we arose with Him. When Christ was seated at the right hand of the Father, we were seated with Him (See Eph. 2:6). In other words, we were made to function in union with Christ. He has already beaten Satan. And you are in union with Him.

> Read Ephesians 6:10-13. According to this passage, why have we been given the full armor of God?

> How is the armor of God related to standing firm in Christ?

God has given you everything you need to see His victory manifested in your life. The means by which we see that victory is through the armor of God. And just as you wouldn't get partially dressed when you wake up in the morning before heading out the door, God doesn't want you to be partially spiritually dressed either.

> Read Ephesians 6:14-17. Which piece of the armor would you think it would be easiest for you to put on?

> Which do you think would be the most difficult? Why?

> Notice the difference between the pieces of armor in verses 14-15 and the pieces in 16-17. How do Paul's commands in what to do with the armor differ in these two sections?

In these verses Paul gives clear instructions about a specific wardrobe that is necessary for us not only to wear but also to have at our disposal when we engage in spiritual warfare.

You might think of it like a travel guide that is provided when you are going somewhere you've never been before. For example, when a person signs up to go on a safari in a remote region of the world, that person can go online and find a travel guide that will give him the details about the recommended articles of clothing and items to bring with them. In the same way, Paul has given us our travel guide so that we will know what to suit up in and take with us into the battle.

Each of the six pieces of armor is divided into one of two categories. The first category includes the first three pieces of armor and begins with the word *with*. This means you should wear the first three pieces at all times. You should never take them off. They are like a uniform a baseball player puts on to play ball.

> Look back at Ephesians 6:14-15. Why do you think these pieces are described as pieces you should never take off?

The last three pieces of the armor are given to you to pick up as the situation demands. We are told to "take" them up. This is like that same baseball player grabbing his glove or his bat at a particular moment in the game.

> Look back at Ephesians 6:16-17. Why do you think these pieces are described as pieces to take up?

Regardless of the armor, though, notice this: God is not going to dress us. He provides what we need, but the responsibility for putting it on is left to us.

It's time to suit up. Game on.

> Pray today for the spiritual insight to put on God's armor as you discover more about it.

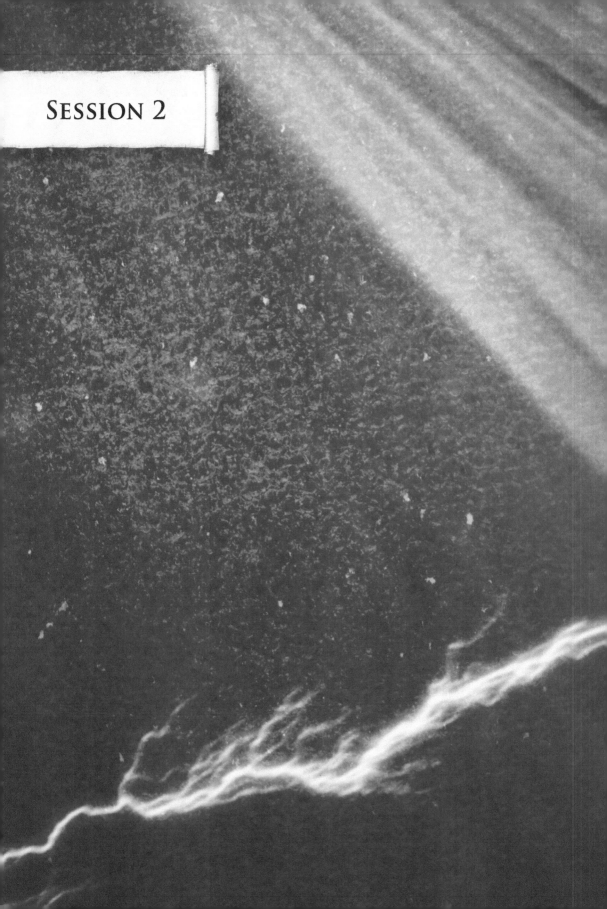

# SESSION 2

# BELT OF TRUTH

## SESSION 2 | THE BELT OF TRUTH

## GETTING STARTED

1. Share one particular insight you gained through your personal devotions this week.

2. Did you find yourself more aware of spiritual conflict around you?

3. Why do you think the first piece of armor is related to the truth? Why might this be an appropriate place to begin armoring yourself for the spiritual battle?

## ARMING UP

**Watch the teaching segment from the DVD using the viewer guide below.**

A belt brings _____ to the rest of the attire.

Truth is an _____ _____ by which reality is measured.

Truth is not predicated on how you _____ or what you _____ about it.

Truth is that which is real ... because it was real _____.

Since God is the originator of all origin, only _____ can be the fixed standard of what is true.

The ultimate question of truth is this: What will be your final _____?

You cannot use your _____ as a measurement of truth.

You cannot use your _____ as a measurement of truth.

You cannot use your _____ _____ as a measurement of truth.

If you have believed a lie, you have invited a _____.

We are to tear down anything that _____ God's point of view from getting through.

"lofty thing"—_____

Anything—regardless of popularity, status, or opinion—that disagrees with a divine _____ of _____ is not the truth.

**Discuss the teaching with your group, using the questions below.**

1. What is the basis for your own standard of truth? Feelings? Opinions of others? Moral instincts?

2. Share an experience when you relied on something other than God for your standard of truth. What were the results?

3. What is one practice you can begin this week to begin to define all of life according to what God says?

**Close with prayer.**

Video sessions available at www.bhpublishinggroup.com/victoryinspiritualwarfare
or with a subscription to smallgroup.com

# GET IN THE FIGHT!

"If you continue in My word, you really are My disciples. You will know the truth, and the truth will set you free." John 8:31-32

Make a list in a journal of all the ways you observe this week that truth is being corrupted. Also, take note of what is influencing you the most in how you define what is true.

As a way of integrating God's truth into your life, carry an index card with you of your memory verse. Periodically review it each day.

# SESSION TWO

My wife, Lois, and I were recently walking in London near Westminster Palace when I noticed a number of people looking down at their watches, making an adjustment, and then looking back up again. This pattern continued for some time.

After a few minutes of this, I realized what they were doing: aligning their personal timepieces with England's timepiece, Big Ben. However, I didn't see anyone approach a guard and tell him that he needed to get whoever was in charge of Big Ben to change its time because it was five minutes off from his watch. To do that would have been ridiculous because everyone in England knows all time must adjust to the true time as declared by Big Ben.

Big Ben doesn't care about anyone else's watch. Big Ben doesn't care how anyone else feels about his or her watch. Big Ben doesn't even care if a lot of people prefer a certain kind of watch or if everyone's watch says the same time. Big Ben is not impressed by how much money someone spent buying his or her watch. Big Ben doesn't take polls to find out what everyone's watch has to say. Big Ben simply tells the time, and everyone is supposed to adjust to Big Ben.

That's how truth is.

*In a day and time when the very concept of truth is under attack, the first piece of armor to strap on is the belt.*

| DAY 1 | WHAT IS THE BELT OF TRUTH? |
|-------|---------------------------|

Paul tells us in Ephesians 2:6-7, "Together with Christ Jesus He also raised us up and seated us in the heavens, so that in the coming ages He might display the immeasurable riches of His grace through His kindness to us in Christ Jesus."

It is in the authority attached to this location that we are to make our stand. To help us stand, the first piece of the wardrobe God has given us to wear at all times as we wage victorious spiritual warfare is a belt.

> Read Ephesians 6:13-14. Why do you think the first piece of armor is a belt?

> What are some reasons you wear a belt?

> Do you think any of those relate to putting on this particular belt? Why or why not?

Like you, I have a number of belts hanging in my closet at home. When I get dressed for the day, I often choose which belt I wear based on its color. But when Paul instructed us to wrap our waists with truth, he wasn't telling us to put on any ordinary belt based on either color or design.

A Roman soldier's belt was a useful tool—a place where some of his other armor could hang. He might hang a sword, dagger, or any number of needed items on his belt. Additionally, when a soldier went into battle, he would tuck the part of his tunic draping near his feet into his belt. By doing so, he would have greater freedom of movement with his feet.

How does the description of the Roman soldier's belt add to your understanding of the spiritual belt?

Why might we need to hang other elements of armor on the belt of truth?

How does truth give you greater freedom of movement in the spiritual battle?

Truth is the beginning point of everything. If there aren't some things in your belief system that you absolutely know to be true, then everything else falls apart. Like a line of dominoes put upright, they all begin tumbling down if the one at the beginning of the line topples over.

It's no wonder putting on the armor starts with truth because it's from a firm conviction about the nature of God, humanity, and the universe from which everything else flows. When we are confident about who God is and the victory He's won in Christ, we are nimble in the battle before us.

Not only did the belt provide the functional ability to hold additional pieces of armor and the freedom for the soldier to be swift in battle through increased mobility, but the belt also produced stability by holding things in place. Essentially, when you or I wear a belt today, we put it on to fulfill two fundamental purposes. Either we want to hold up our pants, or we want to keep our shirts tucked in. We use the belt to stabilize.

Is there any area of your life in which you need stability?

What makes this area of life feel so out of control?

How could truth provide stability to that particular situation?

The belt of truth is designed to stabilize everything else by keeping it all of it in its proper order.

Read the following verses:

Hebrews 6:18
Titus 1:2
Numbers 23:19
1 Samuel 15:29

What theme do they all have in common?

Why is it important to believe that God will not—and cannot—lie?

When a believer understands and operates under the objective nature of God's truth, that truth automatically stabilizes all other areas in life. Jesus said in John 8:32 that "you will know the truth, and the truth will set you free." I often hear Christians quoting this verse, frequently emphasizing the "truth will make you free." But it's not the truth itself that makes you free; it's that you *know* the truth.

The truth that Christians know is the truth that embodies the power to free them. And since God is the only one who can't lie, He is the only one who exists in a state of absolute truth. He is the source not only of our freedom but also of our stability and victory.

Feelings cannot be the standard by which we measure reality. Though important, feelings just aren't always true. Our feelings must always be brought in line with God's truth, or they can guide us down an unstable path. But when we choose to know the One who embodies truth, great things can come from that stability.

Read John 17:17. What did Jesus pray would be the effect of truth?

What image comes to your mind when you read the word *sanctify*?

Jesus goes so far as to pray that the truth would sanctify His followers. To sanctify means *to set apart for special use*. That's what can happen with us. Because of truth, we can find ourselves set apart for special use instead of being beaten down in the spiritual battle.

Problem is, not everyone loves the truth.

Pray today that you will become a person who genuinely loves the truth of God and His Word.

# DAY 2 | THE LIAR

The belt of truth is designed to stabilize things by keeping them in their proper order. This is very important in spiritual battle because Satan is the ultimate twister of truth. Like a magician at a stage show, Satan distorts reality, altering it into any number of shapes and forms. The Bible reveals what we are up against when we face him.

Read John 8:44. According to this passage, how deep is Satan's hatred of the truth?

Why do you think he hates the truth so much?

Think of one time when you believed a lie of the Enemy. Describe it below. What ultimately made you see that this was a lie?

This is a dramatically different picture than what we see from God. It's God's nature to tell the truth; if He ever lied, He would be going against the very core of Himself. Conversely, lying is the most natural thing in the world for Satan. Every time he opens his evil mouth, you can bet that a lie is going to come out.

The difficult part for us in the battle is recognizing the lies. They're so hard to spot because Satan doesn't only lie; he lies very specifically according to whom he's speaking to. The lies of the Enemy are tailor-made and specific according to your own personality. When he confronts you with lies, you will often find they touch you at the deepest levels of insecurity or desire.

That's what makes the lies of the Enemy so appealing. They promise fulfillment and happiness. They seize upon the areas of our lives we think are lacking and promise there's more than we have. And they challenge what we fundamentally believe to be true about God—that He loves us.

Read Genesis 3:1-6. How did Satan twist the truth in these verses?

How was this a challenge to the love of God?

As he did with Eve in the garden, Satan wants to get you to question the value of all the trees that God deemed as acceptable by getting you to focus on the one tree He has said to avoid. The lies of the Enemy cause us to think God has withheld at least some of His blessings from us. In Eve's case it was the fruit from the forbidden tree, but it could be almost anything for you.

It all begins with the challenge of truth. A seemingly small lie. Just a slight deviation from God's revealed Word. Then it progresses into our minds and hearts as we wonder whether God really has our best interests at heart. We wonder how God could love us if He tells us to avoid so many things: *If God loves me, why does He tell me to deny my same-sex attraction? If God loves me, why does He warn me against buying things that will make my family comfortable? If God loves me, why do I have to tell the truth on my tax return when the government is just going to waste my money anyway?*

See how that works? The lies of the Devil make us question the love of God. So how are we to fight the lies? With the belt of truth.

Compare Genesis 3:1-6 to Matthew 4:1-11. How were the temptations of Jesus similar to what we saw in the garden?

How did Jesus combat the lies of the Devil?

If anyone ever had a reason to give in to temptation, it was Jesus. He had been fasting for 40 days and 40 nights when the Devil came to Him and promised Him bread. Then Satan urged Him to do a miracle. He finally told Jesus He should rightfully rule over the kingdoms of the world.

Notice the subtlety of these lies. In each of these cases, the Devil appealed to the core of His target. Jesus is fully man, and because He is, He knows what it's like for His stomach to growl. Satan appealed to His most basic and pressing need at that moment. Surely it couldn't be that God would want His own Son to go hungry, could it?

Jesus also knew He had the power to keep Himself from harm and perform all kinds of other miracles. In fact, part of His mission on earth was to perform those miracles. Wouldn't God want Him to exercise His power like this?

Jesus was destined to be the King of the universe. Wouldn't God want Him to take hold of that destiny and rule over the nations? Each time the Devil took a legitimate desire and corrupted it. But Jesus Christ did what Eve and Adam could not. He spotted the lies of the Devil and put them down with truth.

> How did the Devil respond to Jesus after Jesus conquered the temptations?

> What did Jesus have to believe to be true in order to respond the way He did?

Jesus was absolutely convinced of the goodness and love of His Father. He was so sure of who God was that He was able to stand firm against the ruthless and insidious attacks of the Enemy. If we, like Jesus, want to wear the belt of truth, we must also become convinced of what exactly is true.

> Pray today that you will be able to recognize the seemingly small lies of the Devil.

# DAY 3 — THE TRUTH

"What is truth?" Pilate asked that question more than two thousand years ago (see John 18:38), and people are still wondering about it today. Relativism permeates our culture, asserting that my truth may not be your truth, and your truth may not be your neighbor's truth.

How would you answer Pilate's question?

Why is it important to believe in absolute truth—that truth is not situational in nature?

What are the effects when the nature of truth is attacked?

When people no longer believe in absolute truth, leaving no overarching and guiding truth to which we all subscribe, society is left in a state of constant flux. We live in a similar situation to the one we read about in the Book of Judges: "In those days there was no king in Israel; everyone did whatever he wanted" (Judg. 21:25).

Reflect on that verse. What do you imagine such a time in Israel was like?

How do you see similar tendencies playing out in the world today?

If we want to put on the belt of truth, there are key principles regarding truth that we must embrace. But first know that embracing these principles is a very counter-cultural ambition; here is where we go against the flow. For a Christian engaged in a spiritual battle, there is no room to be unsure about the nature of truth. Unlike the surrounding world, we must stand firm in our belief that God is the origin of truth. As the Creator of truth, He is the only one who knows and understands all truth. Truth, then, is fundamentally God-based knowledge. Truth, at its core, is God's view of a matter.

The first principle of truth, then, is that while truth is composed of information and facts, it also includes original intent. This makes truth the absolute, objective standard by which reality is measured. Often, though, we struggle with this principle because we have all kinds of clever ways to commit to the facts while twisting the intention behind them.

Can you think of an instance when you have been tempted to do this—state the facts and yet not tell the whole truth?

Read Psalm 51:6. How does this verse relate to the previous question?

God wants truth to resonate in our inner self because that is the core from which our intentions flow. When we tell only part of the story and rationalize that we are technically telling the truth, we show that we haven't embraced the first principle of the nature of truth.

The second principle of truth is that truth has already been predetermined by God. This proposition doesn't make sense when a person believes there is no such thing as absolute truth. One plus one equals two. One plus one has always equalled and will always equal two. Even when I don't feel like one plus one equaling two and even if I really feel that I want it to equal three, one plus one will still equal two. Truth can't change simply because we want it to.

> What is one instance in your life when you wanted truth to change
> according to your desires?

The problem is, we want truth to be stable. Suppose you went to a doctor for chest pains and instead of examining you, the doctor put you on some new pills that he *felt* were great. He wasn't exactly sure what they were for, but he said they came with a fancy flyer.

When it comes to things like health, we want to function by a standard of truth. How much more important is it to function by a standard of truth when facing and battling the Enemy, whose mission is to destroy you with lies? Truth is a powerful reality, predetermined by God, that sets the standard with which our thoughts and decisions must align.

A third principle of truth is that truth must resonate internally in order to have any validity externally. Because it is within our spirit where God relates, what is true outside us in our actions must also be true inside our spirit. Internal truth—being honest with our motives, sins, mistakes, beliefs, and desires—is an essential step to strapping on the belt of truth.

Do you know yourself well enough to be honest with God?
Why or why not?

What life experiences have led you to a greater degree of honesty
with yourself?

One way Satan fights truth is by distorting it in our relationships with God. He wants us to go before God as a charade rather than spiritually real. But can I tell you a secret? God knows everything about you. You can't shock or surprise Him. Wearing the belt of truth means being real with God.

If a person can't be truthful with God, who already knows the truth, Satan has stripped that person of the foundational piece of armor before the battle even begins. But living in truth is sometimes easier said than done.

Pray today in the most honest way you can. Ask God, who knows
all things, to search your heart and show you your innermost self.

# DAY 4 | THE OBSTACLES

It sounds simple, doesn't it? Just live by the truth. But how do you know what is true? Most people use one of three things to determine truth: their emotions, their intelligence, or their moral instincts.

Which of these elements would you most likely use to determine truth? Why?

Which would you least likely? Why?

Everybody wants to *feel* that something is true. The problem is that emotions fluctuate and change. If I told you I'm giving you $1 million, your emotions might fly high. But if I then told you the $1 million is in play money, your emotions would crumble to the ground. We need to acknowledge our emotions because they are real, but we also need to acknowledge that our emotions can't always be trusted.

Read Jeremiah 17:9-10. What characteristic of the heart does this passage describe?

What is God's response to the deceitful heart?

Can you think of a situation when you were deceived by your emotions? What did you learn about your emotions from that situation?

What about your intelligence? I'm sure you're very smart. You might have degrees, experience, and common sense. But are you infinite in your brilliance? If you are wondering, think about the last time you changed your mind. We change our minds for one primary reason: we become aware of information we didn't previously have.

The very fact that we change our minds proves the limitations of our knowledge. But what about God? Well, He's the only One who has never said, "Oops."

Read Romans 11:33-36. What characteristic of God inspired Paul's writing of this passage?

Record three examples of how the perfect knowledge of God impacts the way we relate to Him.

1.

2.

3.

Do you use your moral instincts to determine what you believe to be true? Everyone has a built-in moral compass, but even that can change based on emotions, new information, outside influences, and maturity. We often find that our internal moral compass shifts, depending on our life circumstances. This shifting invalidates it as a source of objective truth.

Can you think of one instance when your moral instincts have changed when you have either hardened or softened a moral stance on a subject?

What caused the change?

What, then, will be the standard of truth? In what will you place your trust, ultimately defining reality? I hate to tell you this, but you can't trust you. And you can't trust me. Why? Because our souls, minds, wills, and emotions have been distorted. Have you ever been to an amusement park and looked in the mirrors that make you look fat, tall, or skinny? The deepest parts of who we are have become distorted like these mirrors. The penetrating effects of sin have reached into our souls and twisted them so that they can no longer be recognized as what they were created to be.

A person looking into a carnival mirror could not accurately describe the true person who is being reflected in the mirror. Neither can you accurately define truth when looking through the lens of your soul. The soul within you, your viewpoint on a matter, needs to be restored through the truth of God.

Read Hebrews 4:12-13. What parts of the description of Scripture in this passage line up with your view of Scripture?

What parts of the description challenge you?

Have you ever experienced a time when the Word of God felt like a sword to your soul? When?

The Bible is God's revelation of Himself. It's truth recorded for all time. The Word of God provides us with the ultimate standard of truth. But it's more than stale words on a page.

The writer of Hebrews describes Scripture as "living and effective" and says it divides "soul and spirit" and judges "the ideas and thoughts of the heart" (v. 12). That's what we need. The Bible, through the power of the Holy Spirit, has the capability not only of telling us what we ought to believe is true but also of showing us our own deficiencies in the way we are currently defining truth.

If we approach Scripture not with presumption but with an open heart, asking God to reveal our true motives and thoughts, we'll find stability in its pages. God will show us what truth is—truth that goes beyond what we think or feel.

That's how we start to put on the belt of truth.

Pray today for an open heart to the Word of God. Ask God to make His Word living and active in your life.

# DAY 5 | PUTTING ON THE BELT

We cannot trust ourselves to define truth. Truth begins and ends with God. He's the Author of truth, and He's incapable of lying. Our viewpoint on a given matter needs to be restored by exchanging our thoughts with God's truth. In fact, much of what we battle takes place right between our ears. The first step to fighting those battles, then, is found in our minds.

Read Romans 12:2. What is the result of renewing our minds, according to this verse?

What are you currently putting into your mind that might prevent this renewal from happening?

The renewal of the mind is a commitment to agree with God about the nature of truth and all reality. That's how we put on the belt, and the Holy Spirit is right there, helping to make it happen.

Read 1 Corinthians 2:10-12. What does the Holy Spirit do, according to this passage?

The Greek word Paul uses for *searches* in this passage is the word *eruna*, which means *to continually examine something*.[1] In this case the Holy Spirit is continually examining everything—even the depths of God.

According to verse 12, what do we gain from the Holy Spirit?

Have you ever thought of the Spirit as granting us that kind of information? If not, what do you usually think of the Holy Spirit doing?

The Spirit gives us the ability to know God and His truth, and that knowledge gives us the ability to walk in victory in our day-to-day lives. But note that we gain the ability to know God. The Holy Spirit never forces us to know God or be renewed by His truth. But it is through the work of the Spirit that we are given the opportunity to exchange our viewpoint with God's. This exchange is a key aspect of wearing the belt of truth.

Read 2 Corinthians 10:3-5. Paul writes that we take "every thought captive to obey Christ." How does taking our thoughts captive lead to obedience to Jesus?

What kinds of thoughts are most difficult for you to capture? Lust? Greed? Jealousy? Anger?

God reveals one of Satan's strategies through this passage. Satan seeks to set up speculations (or wrong thoughts) in our minds that contradict God's truth. This includes anything that inhibits, distorts, or alters God's viewpoint on a matter. It could be something that seems as harmless as your mother's opinion about what you should do or think. It could be what your friends or the media are persuading you to do or believe. It could even be your own thoughts generated from the distortion of your soul.

How, specifically, has your sense of truth been altered by the following groups?

Family:

Friends:

Media:

Coworkers:

Do you define romance based on the latest movie you saw? Do you define hard work and ambition based on your boss's definition? Do you define success based on the achievements of your parents? Satan doesn't care whether you mix some of God's truth in with the rest of the truth you're gathering from other sources. He knows if he can twist what you believe to be true, that will be enough to set up speculations and raise lofty things against the knowledge of God.

That's the sneaky way Satan tries to strip us of the belt of truth. He says, "Go to church. Read your Bible. Memorize your verses. As a matter of fact, even I quote those verses (out of their contextual truth). But at the end of the day, sprinkle in a little about what the world says, what your parents say, how your friends think, what the television portrays, or whatever else you feel, desire, or want to believe."

Satan knows that when you've done that, you've taken off your own belt. He didn't have to take it off for you.

*What is one area of influence you need to remove from your life in order to more fully align yourself with God's truth?*

*What is one practice you need to incorporate into your life in order to be renewing your mind with God's truth?*

When you wear the belt of truth and operate with it by aligning your mind, will, and emotions underneath God's view on a matter, He will enable you to fight your spiritual battles with the freedom of greater mobility and increased stability. By knowing and functioning according to the truth of God, you will be on your way to experiencing victory over anything seeking to defeat you.

*Pray today for the renewing of your mind. Infuse your prayers with the promises of God found in Scripture.*

1. Spiros Zodhiates, *The Complete Word Study New Testament with Greek Parallel* (Chattanooga, TN: AMG Publishers, 1992), 33.

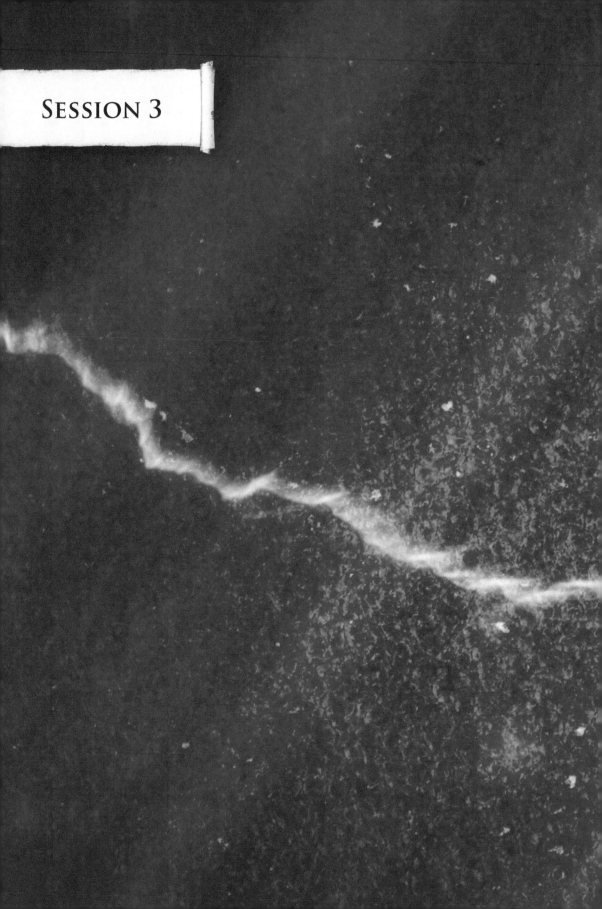

# BREASTPLATE OF RIGHTEOUSNESS

# SESSION 3

# THE BREASTPLATE OF RIGHTEOUSNESS

## GETTING STARTED

1. Share one particular insight you gained through your personal devotions this week.

2. What area of your life would most dramatically change if you completely lived according to God's truth?

3. The next piece of spiritual armor is the breastplate of righteousness. How would you define righteousness?

## ARMING UP

**Watch the teaching segment from the DVD using the viewer guide below.**

Righteousness is the _____ God requires for people to become acceptable to Him.

Righteousness is the _____ of truth in the life of the believer.

Demons function on _____.

Unrighteousness _____ the demonic flow and _____ the move of God.

The first three pieces of armor are meant to be worn _____ the _____.

A breastplate protects the chest which contains the _____.

The heart is the spiritual pump that pumps the _____ of God into you.

Religion will only help to _____ sin.

God has already _____ a righteous seed within you.

_____ occurs when the truth of God is meditated on and righteousness is released from the spirit.

The Word of God is a _____ that tells you the truth about who you are.

Released righteousness makes you righteous in the heart as well as _____.

At salvation, God deposited within your soul all the righteousness of _____ _____. But you must be willing to dig it up.

**Discuss the teaching with your group, using the questions below.**

1. What is the relationship between your personal righteousness and the righteousness given to you in Christ?

2. Why is righteousness linked to a piece of armor that protects your heart?

3. Why is it necessary to put on the belt of truth before you put on the breastplate of righteousness?

**Close with prayer.**

Video sessions available at www.bhpublishinggroup.com/victoryinspiritualwarfare or with a subscription to smallgroup.com

59

# GET IN THE FIGHT!

**Scripture Memory:**

> "He made the One who did not know sin
> to be sin for us, so that we might become
> the righteousness of God in Him."
> 2 Corinthians 5:21

- Spend time each day this week in prayer thanking God specifically for the righteousness of Christ that has been given to you.

- Also spend time each day confessing the sin in your life, cleansing yourself of the unrighteousness of thought and deed.

# SESSION THREE

I'm responsible for taking out the trash in our home. Because I am, I purchased a machine called a trash masher. I love my trash masher. It will give me at least one extra day before I have to empty the kitchen trash. Depending on how many people are in the house, it might even give me two.

The problem with my trash masher is that it is no match for my wife's standards. Lois can smell day-old trash even before it's a day old. She doesn't want any smell permeating the home that she spends so much time making comfortable for us, so she'll ask me, "Tony, did you forget about the trash?"

Lois knows that even smashed trash is smelly trash.

Let's say that I go against the wishes of my wife and keep smashing the trash instead of taking it out. The house would still be our house. The trash police wouldn't come and claim my deed as their own. But having that trash there, even if it's smashed, creates an environment for roaches and ants to come and live. It's almost like putting down a welcome mat for your new guests. The roaches will invite their cousins and make themselves at home.

Putting on the breastplate of righteousness deals with both issues above. The righteousness of Christ secures your deed to the home. And putting on the breastplate makes sure no demons come in and make themselves comfortable.

*If you're smelling the trash today,*
*it's time to put on the breastplate.*

# WHAT IS THE BREASTPLATE OF RIGHTEOUSNESS?

## DAY 1

Once we are fitted with the belt of truth, Paul advises us to proceed with the next item in the spiritual wardrobe. He says we should take up "righteousness like armor on your chest" (Eph. 6:14).

Keep in mind that Paul was writing this letter not as a free man but in chains, under guard from Roman authorities. Perhaps as he sat in his jail cell, penning these words to the church at Ephesus, he looked through the bars and observed the guard standing there. He noticed the belt that held everything in place. Then he saw a metal plate that was worn over a coat of chain mail to protect the chest and back. This, to Paul, is what righteousness does for a believer.

If you were a soldier, why might you want to wear a piece of armor like this?

Why would you feel protected when wearing a breastplate?

The soldier needed a breastplate like this primarily to protect the heart. Why should we want to protect our hearts? Because the only reason the rest of our body can operate is because of the heart. Once the heart stops, everything else stops too. This is true not only in the physical realm but also in the spiritual realm.

Read Proverbs 4:23. How does this verse describe the heart?

How is the heart, in a spiritual sense, similar to the heart in a physical sense?

As the heart is the physical pump controlling the flow of blood throughout our body, the heart, our essence and our core, is the spiritual pump that God uses to infuse life into us. When we became Christians, the Holy Spirit took up residence in our hearts. The work of the Spirit within us is to pump life into our souls so that eventually the Spirit becomes the dominant influencer in what we feel, think, and do.

Religion often tries to change a person from the outside. Religion tells us that we will be more victorious if we go to church more, give more, serve more, and be an all-around better person. But authentic victory happens on the inside, when the Spirit of God pumps God's truth throughout the different areas of our life. As a heart pumps blood, the Spirit pumps the truth of God to the soul. The soul then tells the body to adjust to God's standard instead of its own.

That brings us to how the breastplate of righteousness relates to the belt of truth.

How might righteousness relate to truth?

It's appropriate that the breastplate of righteousness comes right after the belt of truth. Truth is God's view on a matter. It establishes the basis of our reality. It's more substantial than our feelings, opinions, or circumstances. In the end, what we think doesn't matter—we must align our thoughts with God's truth. Acknowledging, accepting, and believing God's view on a matter gives our whole lives stability.

The belt of truth comes before the breastplate of righteousness because there can't be righteousness apart from truth. Truth sets the standard. Righteousness reveals how to work that standard out. Or to put it another way, righteousness is the response to truth.

Consider the following issues. Record God's opinion for each of the topics:

Sex:

Food:

Money:

God's opinion of sex, for example, is that it is good. Sex is designed to be an act between one man and one woman in the context of marriage. Righteousness, then, is how we respond to that truth.

God gave us food to enjoy and sustain our bodies. Righteousness is how we respond to that truth. If we eat like gluttons who will never have another meal, we reveal our unrighteousness because we are not responding to God's revealed truth.

But righteousness goes deeper than just action. Like truth, which includes more than facts but also the intention behind them, righteousness includes more than right behavior. A person might—and often does—have the right behavior and yet contaminates it with the wrong motivation.

Can you think of any characters in Scripture who displayed this kind of righteousness?

What was God's response to them?

That was the issue with the Pharisees. Great behavior. Awful motivation. They were like a young boy who was told by his teacher to sit down. He didn't want to sit, but he knew there would be consequences if he didn't. So he sat. But in his heart he was saying, *Even though I'm sitting down on the outside, I'm standing up on the inside.*

Unlike the teacher, who couldn't see the boy's heart, God sees deep within us and measures the motivation of all we do or don't do. That presents us with a very serious problem in the area of righteousness.

Pray for your heart. Acknowledge that the heart is where spiritual life comes from. Ask Him to conform your inner desires to His.

# DAY 2 — RIGHTEOUSNESS

*Righteousness* simply means *being or doing what is right.* The breastplate comes after the belt of truth because there can't be righteousness apart from truth. The standard of truth is revealed, and we respond.

Here's the problem though. Not a single one of us has responded appropriately.

> Read Romans 3:10-12. This passage addresses how far-reaching sin is in the world. How long is the reach of sin, according to this passage?

> Read Romans 8:19-22. How much impact does sin have on the world?

Sin is more than just doing the wrong thing or responding inappropriately to the revelation of truth. When we choose wrong, we sin, but sin goes deeper. We are sinful by nature. Our hearts are inclined toward evil. Sin is, in fact, the root issue of all the world's problems, whether its prostitution, gambling, or even earthquakes.

Left to our own devices, we are going to consistently choose sin instead of righteousness. Is it even possible, then, for us to put on this breastplate? By the power of God in Christ, it is indeed. But we must understand that there are two sides to righteousness—the being side and the doing side.

> Paul describes the being side of righteousness in 2 Corinthians 5:21. According to this verse, what have we received because of Christ? What has Christ received in return?

Everyone who has trusted in Jesus Christ for the forgiveness of their sins has been imputed with righteousness. That means that the righteousness of Jesus—His perfect day-to-day life, along with His faultless motives—have been credited to our account. God not only removed the stain of sin when you trusted in Jesus Christ, but He also replaced that stain with the righteous standard of Christ. So now when God looks at you, He sees you as equal to His Son.

He doesn't just see someone who has been forgiven of his or her sins; He sees someone who has kept the full standard of righteousness.

Have you ever thought about yourself in those terms? Why or why not?

How might your attitude toward sin change if you thought of yourself as having the righteousness of Christ?

Imputing righteousness can be compared to God's crediting your account or putting money in your bank. The money now belongs to you. No one can take that money away from you—not even Satan. Once you are saved, Satan can do nothing to change your righteous standing before God. This is called justification.

However, because Satan can't take away your imputed righteousness, he tries to restrict your personal practice. You personal practice is the other side of righteousness—the doing side.

What do you think is the proper relationship between being righteous and doing righteousness?

We are meant to act in accordance with our new being in Christ. Or to put it another way, we are to work out what God has worked in. We are already righteous in standing; now we are to choose to be righteous in practice.

Satan tries to bring a breach between our position of righteousness and our practice of righteousness. When he is successful, there is broken fellowship between God and us.

That is why Paul instructs us to put on the breastplate of righteousness. To that end, he also instructs us to put something else on.

Read Titus 2:10. What are we told in this passage to adorn?

When you adorn something, you wear it—you put it on. You dress up with it and look better because of it. God instructs us to dress up with doctrine. What is the doctrine of God? It's fundamentally the truth of God revealed through Scripture. To practice righteousness through adorning truth involves abstaining "from fleshly desires that war against you" (1 Pet. 2:11). It means being fully covered not only in positional righteousness but also in the personal practice of righteous behavior.

We wear the breastplate when we are fully convinced of our righteous position because of Christ. We take this on faith, and that faith influences our practice. We then choose to live out of that righteousness. The inner righteous position begins to flow into our outer righteous practice.

But rest assured: even though he has no power over us, thanks to Jesus, Satan is the great accuser who wants to bring charges against both our position and practice.

Pray today, thanking God for making you righteous in Christ. Ask for help in believing that truth, and pray that your faith will impact your practice of righteousness.

THE ACCUSER

I think we would be surprised if we learned to view sin the way God views sin. For example, we read in the Book of 1 John that God elevates hatred to the level of murder.

Read 1 John 3:15. Compare that verse to Matthew 5:21-22. Do you typically take sin as seriously as God does? Why or why not?

Why do you think we tend to minimize sin as Christians?

Apparently, there are a lot of convicted felons coming to church every week—many not even aware of the gravity God places on sin. Keeping us unaware of our own sin is one of Satan's strategies in spiritual warfare because he knows we will not confess what we do not recognize.

Even though we see the seriousness of sin here in 1 John, we also find the good news that God can remove that stain and stench of sin from us.

Read 1 John 1:8-9. What is the promise in these verses?

If God already knows about our sin, why does He desire confession?

No one on earth is without sin. Sin manifests itself in many different varieties. There are overt sins—sins that are done outwardly through our actions. There are covert sins, which take place in our minds, hearts, and emotions. There are also sins of commission, which are knowingly carried out. Finally, there are sins of omission—these are things we should do but choose not to.

God knows about all of these sins. He knows about the sinful actions and the sinful motivations behind those actions. But He nonetheless desires confession. Why?

Before answering that question, we should acknowledge that Satan loves sin. More than that, he loves unconfessed sin.

Read Zechariah 3:1-5. What was the high priest's problem in this passage?

How was the problem remedied?

What was Satan doing in this passage?

A preacher named Joshua came before the Lord with dirty clothes on. He came before God displaying his unrighteousness. But he didn't do what many of us do when we sin—try and hide our dirty clothes or try and persuade God to believe that our clothes aren't really as dirty as they appear. That's what Satan would have liked Joshua to do.

Read Revelation 12:10. How are Satan's actions in this passage similar to his actions in the passage above?

When are the times you hear Satan's accusing voice most clearly?

Satan's number one hobby is to accuse us of all of the wrong things we have ever done or thought. In the face of those accusations, the temptation is to run and hide rather than do what Joshua did. Confessing our sin to God is telling Him something He already knows. But it's through confession and hearing His pronouncement of forgiveness that we'll restore our practice of righteousness back into alignment with our position of righteousness.

We underestimate the power of coming clean with God. Too often our prayers focus on how God can bless us, take care of us, protect us, and deliver us, even when He has given us the key to victory through one critical move—confession.

Doing wrong is wrong—sin is sin. However, unconfessed sin breeds an even greater environment for it to continue. Unrighteousness and disobedience unlock a door that allows Satan and his demons to enter, influence, and take control of the environment.

But when we confess our sin, God promises cleansing. That's why Joshua stood before God. He was open about his failings and believed in God's power to take care of it.

Look back at the story in Zechariah 2. What, specifically, did God replace Joshua's dirty clothes with?

God responded to Joshua's dirty clothes and Satan's accusation by removing his iniquity and covering him instead with clothes designed for a unique and special purpose. These were festal robes. Joshua hadn't done anything to deserve the ability to wear the festal robes. God gave him these robes out of mercy.

He's willing to do the same thing for us, even in our failings. When we are honest with God, He will cleanse us from unrighteousness. We'll be dressed for the party instead of dressed for defeat.

Spend your prayer time today confessing. Ask God to search your heart, and when He does, be open and honest with Him about what He reveals to you.

# INSIDE OUT

We will never experience victory in our practice of righteousness until we fully embrace the victory Christ won for our position of righteousness. These two sides of righteousness are vitally linked together.

Religion doesn't recognize that link, though. Religion often tries to change a person from the outside. Religion tells us we will be victorious if we go to church more, be a better person, give more, serve more, sing louder, or try harder. But that simply produces more and more weary and defeated Christians.

God's plan is not to change us from the outside in but from the inside out.

Read Philippians 2:12. If you read only this verse, what does Paul seem to be saying about the way we are saved?

Now read verse 13. Describe the tension between these two verses.

How might these verses, taken together, relate to righteousness from the inside out?

We might be tempted to look at Philippians 2:12 as something like soul management. That's not a bad thing; I wouldn't want a murderer walking around doing whatever he wanted to. We would all want him to manage his impulses. But just managing impulses doesn't get us to the freedom and abundant life God promises.

We need something deeper. We need soul restoration.

Soul management may stop you from doing something you shouldn't be doing, but it hasn't done anything to fix the fact that you *want* to do it. Far too many of us have settled for behavior modification. This only creates hypocrisy; we look spiritually "well-done" on the outside but are "raw" on the inside.

We must read Philippians 2:12 alongside Philippians 2:13. Who is doing the work in verse 12?

Who is doing the work in verse 13?

There is a causal relationship between these two verses. God is at work within us, and because He is, we work on the outside. In Christ, God fixes our insides. He returns our desires, our thoughts, and our mind-set to the standard He intended them to be in the garden.

We work to live on the outside what He has already done on the inside. We access the perfect righteousness placed within us in order to live righteously on the outside. The Book of James talks about how this process works.

Read James 1:21. What are we to receive, according to this verse?

In what spirit are we to receive it?

The first point we need to recognize from this verse is that James is writing to believers. A few verses earlier he called them "dearly loved brothers" (Jas. 1:19). But even though they are saved, James is still saying their souls need to be saved. James is referring to the process called sanctification, which simply means *becoming more and more like Jesus and less and less like the world.*

Yet in order for sanctification to occur, the soul needs to receive the Word implanted in us. This is when the Holy Spirit's presence is enabled in our lives.

One reason we don't experience victory in spiritual warfare is that we are trying to force on ourselves a man-made breastplate of righteousness. Instead, we must submit humbly to God's truth as the standard of righteousness.

The best scenario I know, which illustrates how we receive this implanted Word within our spirit, is a fertilized egg inside the womb of a woman. When the egg is planted inside the uterus, it will receive, from the mother, the needed nourishment to produce growth. The more nourishment the egg receives, the more the baby grows and becomes dominant in the mother's womb. This continues until eventually the baby dictates all of the mind, will, and emotions of a woman. Eventually, the baby even dictates the entire physical body of the mother during delivery.

Likewise, the righteousness of God, made known through His Word, must reach from His Spirit into our spirit, feeding it as it grows to dominate your soul. As the Word of God feeds your spirit and it begins to influence your soul, your actions will begin to naturally reflect God's viewpoint on a matter.

Are you seeking to find nourishment for your soul in the Bible?

If not, where do you typically find it?

Over time you'll begin to see your desires, wants, and propensities organically change as they become influenced by the Spirit's presence of truth and righteousness within you. Inside out righteousness is what the breastplate is predicated on.

Pray today for a greater hunger for the Word of God.

# Day 5

# Putting on the Breastplate

True righteousness is released, not manufactured. That's why you can only change your practice of righteousness only by understanding your position of righteousness.

Feeding the righteousness planted within you will take more than a minute. It means meditating on, rehearsing, and considering over and over again the truths found in God's Word. You should *fantasize* about God's truth. You read that right—fantasize about what God says in His Word. Let it become just as real to you in your thoughts as the realness of the world all around you. Just as the act of worrying about something can actually make the thing you are worrying about seem worse over time, fantasizing about the righteous truths and promises of God revealed in His Word will make them more real to you.

How much time do you spend, in an average week, really examining the Bible?

What are the top three obstacles you face during that time?

1.

2.

3.

Living in victory requires replacing the deceptions of Satan and the distortions in your soul with the righteousness of God found in His truth. As you begin to receive the truth of God's Word, your soul begins to speak to your body about practical areas of righteousness: "You have to walk differently. You have to think differently. You have to talk differently. You have to spend differently. You have to, because you are different."

Read Colossians 3:1-5. List below the things Paul says have already happened to you in Christ.

How, according to verse 5, are you to respond to these truths?

The word *therefore* is a powerful one. It means *because of* or *in light of*. Paul is saying that when Christ died, the Christians died. And when He was raised, the Christians were raised. Thanks to Jesus, we are raised into a position of righteousness. The proper response is to live out that righteousness.

Paul says we have already died to sin and death. That means those things have no power over us. We respond now by dying day after day. We access our inner righteous standing and then apply it to things of the world like sexual immorality, impurity, lust, evil desires, and greed.

77

The breastplate of righteousness has been deposited within us. It is our job to feed it and nourish it by reminding ourselves of it, with the truth of God, so that it expands to surround us with the protection we desperately need in warfare.

Read Proverbs 28:1. According to this passage, what do the wicked do?

How about the righteous?

Why do you think the wicked flee even though no one is pursuing them?

What about the righteous? What enables them to be bold?

If I told you I buried $10 million behind your house, you would put down this book right now and make every effort to get a shovel and get to your backyard. You're going to leave wherever you are and quickly go tear up your grass. You're going to dig as deep as you need to dig because the thing you are digging for has life-impacting value. Every effort you put forth to get to that $10 million will be worth it in your mind.

When you were saved by grace and through faith, God deposited deep down within you all of the righteousness that belongs to Christ. But you can't benefit from its restoring abilities unless you're willing to dig down deep with the shovel of truth. If you do, God will release a brand-new you surrounded by the secure protection of a breastplate of His righteousness.

That kind of righteousness makes you bold. It makes you fearless. You can face the Enemy because you are covered with the impenetrable breastplate of righteousness. You don't have to run around naked any more like the wicked do; they sense their vulnerability and are jumping at shadows.

Wearing the breastplate of righteousness involves walking securely in your imputed righteousness by virtue of the cross, coming clean with God in your practice of righteousness, and feeding your spirit with the Word of God so that the Holy Spirit will produce the natural outgrowth of right living within you.

Pray today that your position of righteousness will begin to align with your practice of righteousness as you put on the breastplate.

SESSION 4

# SHOES OF THE GOSPEL OF PEACE

# SESSION 4

# THE SHOES OF THE GOSPEL OF PEACE

## GETTING STARTED

1. Share one particular insight you gained through your personal devotions this week.

2. Why does your personal righteousness serve as protection for your heart?

3. The next pieces of armor are the shoes of the gospel of peace. What is the gospel?

## ARMING UP

**Watch the teaching segment from the DVD using the viewer guide below.**

"preparation"—_____

The Roman soldier's shoes were outfitted with spikes that gave him
_____ _____ when under attack.

The purpose of the shoes is to create _____ for the Christian in the day of evil.

The purpose of the spiritual attack is to keep your salvation from being _____ in your reality.

The opposite of peace is _____.

The biblical definition of peace is calm and tranquility of soul despite _____ _____.

"rule"—_____

Let the peace of God "_____ the _____" in your life.

God will show you what to do once you are operating on the truth
you know by giving you a _____ about the decision.

If _____ is your normal way of operating, you are not wearing the shoes.

The world can only give you _____ peace.

Peace that Jesus is giving away is in the _____.

"gospel"—_____ _____

The gospel refers to the death and resurrection of Jesus Christ
as a _____ for our sins.

Most Christians apply the gospel only to what it takes to get to _____.

We know the gospel because of Jesus' _____, but we have missed
the gospel of His _____.

The goal isn't to try and get something new; it's to _____ _____
what God has already deposited.

**Discuss the teaching with your group, using the questions below.**

1. Share an experience when you would have liked to have been more
   spiritually stable.

2. How does understanding the gospel bring peace?

3. In what one situation in your life right now are you longing for peace?

**Close with prayer.**

Video sessions available at www.bhpublishinggroup.com/victoryinspiritualwarfare
or with a subscription to smallgroup.com

# Get in the Fight!

**Scripture Memory:**

"Don't worry about anything, but in everything, through prayer and petition with thanksgiving, let your requests be made known to God. And the peace of God, which surpasses every thought, will guard your hearts and minds in Christ Jesus." Philippians 4:6-7

- Send an email to your Bible study group this week asking them to pray with you concerning a situation causing you anxiety. Commit to do the same for them.

- Each time you find yourself worrying about something, quote the previous verses to yourself.

# SESSION FOUR

You've probably seen or at least heard about the 1994 Academy Award-winning blockbuster *Forrest Gump*. The film captivated audiences with its ability to capture the nuances of a unique character named Forrest. The first scene in the movie depicts Forrest sitting on a bench in a town square next to a local nurse.

He begins a conversation with her like this: "Those must be comfortable shoes. I bet you could walk all day in shoes like that and not feel a thing. I wish I had shoes like that. Mama always said there's an awful lot you can tell about a person by their shoes. Where they're going. Where they've been. ..."[1]

Shoes play an important role in our lives. They can stand as a symbol, like Dorothy's ruby slippers or Cinderella's glass one. Frequently women, and sometimes men, have obsessions with shoes, as in the notable cases of Imelda Marcos, Eva Peron, or former Romanian President Nicolae Ceausescu. At times in the Old Testament, when God would address people in His presence, He would tell them to remove their shoes.

Not surprisingly, then, our next piece of armor necessary when experiencing spiritual warfare involves footwear.

*After all, you can tell a lot about a person by their shoes.*

# DAY 1

# WHAT ARE THE SHOES?

Paul gives us our next piece of armor to suit up with in Ephesians 6:15: "Your feet sandaled with readiness for the gospel of peace." The word *sandaled*, sometimes translated as *shod*, is used in this statement to refer to what you have on.[2] So according to Paul you not only need to wear the belt of truth and the breastplate of righteousness—you also need to put on your shoes.

> What are some reasons you put your shoes on every day?

> Can you see any correlation between this reasoning and why you would need to put on the spiritual shoes?

A Roman soldier's shoes were called *caliga*. They were sandals heavily studded with nails. These nails were firmly placed directly through the sole of the shoe not only to increase durability but also to increase stability.[3] Similar to cleats worn on football and soccer fields today, these early "cleats" provided traction when needed. This traction kept the soldier—much as they keep a football or soccer player today—from slipping and sliding. Traction gives a person sure footing, making him mobile in battle while at the same time making him more difficult to knock down.

> Given the above description, why might Paul have seen shoes as an essential piece of spiritual armor?

Why does a Christian need great stability and mobility?

When Paul instructs you to put on these shoes, he is talking about the ability to stand firm in a stationary position. This gives you traction so that when Satan comes, he can't knock you off your feet. In fact, you're able to stand firm, because the nails coming out of your peace shoes have dug down deep into the foundation beneath you.

What sorts of things might cause a Christian to be knocked around in life? Recount one time below when you felt that way.

How would you have responded to the situation described above if you had greater stability and mobility?

We all know what it's like to be knocked over from time to time. We know what it's like when circumstances, situations, relationships, finances, careers, or any number of things remove us from our position of stability. These things often happen, causing us to feel unstable, shaky, and defeated.

But Paul is telling us that it doesn't have to be that way.

Read Ephesians 4:11-14. Why, according to verses 12-13, has Jesus gifted specific people in the church with different gifts?

What will happen to Christians when they grow into maturity
(see v. 14)?

A mature Christian is a stable Christian. Jesus Christ has uniquely gifted leaders in the church to instruct people in the gospel so that they can grow up and not be tossed around anymore. See, these shoes aren't just any shoes—these are the shoes of the gospel of peace. When you put them on, you don't have to slide or move with every hit or trial. Shodding your feet with these shoes creates a stability that even Satan can't undo.

When you're unstable, you're always on the defensive. That's just how Satan wants us. When you're on the defensive, you're constantly focused on fending off attacks and never taking the fight to the darkness itself. These shoes are one way you regain your footing and begin to move from defense to offense.

The Greek word for *readiness* in Ephesians 6:15 is *hetoimasia,* which means *promptness* and *speediness.* It is similar in nature to the instruction given to us in 1 Peter 3:15: "Always be ready to give a defense to anyone who asks you for a reason for the hope that is in you."

In these times when nothing is stable—not economies, not health, not families, nothing—someone standing firm will likely get noticed. People might say, "Why are you so confident when job losses are at an all-time high? Why are you calm when there are wars and rumors of wars? What makes you sure when everyone else is not?" These are questions that come when we shod our feet with the gospel of peace.

But let's make sure we know the exact makeup of these shoes if we're going to put them on.

Pray and express to God your desire for stability. Confess that stability can be found only in Him.

# DAY 2 | THE GOSPEL

We have been instructed to put on the shoes of "the gospel of peace" (Eph. 6:14). The Greek word for *gospel* is *euangelion*, which translated simply means *good news*.

The word *euangelion* was frequently used in the New Testament, but rarely used in either classical or koine (common) Greek. The reason it wasn't used in either formal or informal Greek is that the definition of the term referred to news that was so good it was too good to be true. It was a special word for special usage. That's why its importance is felt so heavily when it's used in the Bible. What comes packaged in the gospel is so good that it's too good to be true.

What is the gospel? Define the gospel in two sentences below.

Why it is important to have a firm, succinct definition of the gospel stored in your mind?

At the heart of the gospel are the death and resurrection of Jesus Christ as the substitute for our sins. Here's the problem, though. Most people look at the gospel as the means by which we begin the Christian life, and we then move past it. We get that heaven-and-hell thing taken care of and can get on with the business of living. It's true that the gospel is about getting to heaven, but it also has an awful lot to do with earth.

Read Romans 5:6-10. When, according to this passage, did Christ die for us?

Why is that significant?

Now read Colossians 2:6-7. Rewrite verse 6 in your own words below.

The gospel tells us that while we were sinners, Jesus died for us. He didn't wait for us to clean up our acts; He took the initiative, coming from heaven to earth, to bear the weight of our sin on the cross. This truth isn't something we are meant to get over; it's instead meant to be the fuel from which we live the rest of our lives.

The gospel is the start of the Christian life, but it's also what drives us on in the Christian life. Sanctification, just as much as justification, is fueled by a firm belief and understanding of the gospel.

Read 1 Thessalonians 5:23. Who is responsible for sanctification?

List the elements being sanctified from the verse above:

_____     _____     _____

The word *Himself* in this verse is being used as a reflexive pronoun, indicating that God will sanctify you apart from anyone else's help. Furthermore, notice the progression in which God sanctifies: from spirit to soul to body. God doesn't start with the body and then go to the soul, only to wind up at the spirit. He starts at the spirit to nourish and grow its influence over the soul, which then brings about a change in the body.

At salvation God deposited within each of us a new nature—that is our spirit. The spirit contains all of God's power, presence, peace, and much more. Everything God has in store for you is resident in the new spirit within, and it is perfect. That's what the gospel tells us.

The problem is, your perfect spirit is lodged within your imperfect soul and body. The gospel tells us God will continue that progression of sanctification throughout your entire being. That's why growing in Christ, from justification to sanctification to glorification, is all about the gospel.

Now think back to what you learned yesterday about the purpose of shoes. Why, given what you have read today, would the shoes be linked to the gospel?

How might the gospel provide the kind of stability and mobility we need in the fight?

Everyone has a distorted soul that leads to distorted actions in the body. Our bodies do the wrong things because they are operating off the direction of our distorted souls. This is an important point to realize: you can't fix you.

That's why New Year's resolutions rarely last because they all involve attempts at managing the mess through external means. But God and the gospel don't work like that. God works from the spirit first, then to the soul, and finally to the body.

The gospel gives us stability in that we can time and time again, no matter what we've done wrong, return to the core truth: Jesus died for us. When He did, He made us new. This serves as a reset for our spirits, which influences our souls and ultimately our bodies.

That's why the shoes aren't just any shoes. They're the shoes of the gospel. It's this gospel that can bring us real peace.

> Pray today that you will have a greater and deeper love for understanding of the gospel.

# DAY 3 | PEACE

It seems today we see the word *peace* thrown around all over the place. The popular peace symbol can be found on jewelry, bumper stickers, clothing, notebooks, tattoos, and television advertisements. In the Middle East, peace means the absence of war. To a stay-at-home mother of three small children, it means nap time. To experience victory in spiritual warfare with the shoes fitted with the gospel of peace, you need to understand and wear God's peace.

Define *peace*.

How do you think God would define *peace*? Is there a difference between His definition and yours? Why?

Why is it important that we understand peace from God's perspective?

The Greek word translated as *peace* in Scripture is *eirene*. This word is equivalent to the Hebrew word *shalom*. Essentially, eirene embodies completeness, wholeness, and an inner resting of the soul that does not fluctuate because of outside influences. A person at peace is someone who is stable, calm, orderly, and at rest within. The opposite of peace, of course, reveals itself in inner chaos, anxiety, and worry.

Is the previous definition of peace appealing to you? Which part, specifically?

How closely does your life resemble that life of peace?

What are three things that most often intrude on your sense of peace?

1.

2.

3.

True peace is not dependent on circumstances. Anyone can feel a sense of peace on a beautiful day, reflecting on their perfect health and overflowing bank accounts. But life doesn't work like that.

Real peace doesn't mean there is calm when all is calm. When all is calm, you are supposed to be calm. Godly peace means that you are at rest even when everything else is all wrong.

Thunder and lightning might be chasing each other all around you. The wind could be blowing unexpected and unpleasant circumstances into your life. Nothing looks right. Nothing looks promising. All is dark. But it is exactly in those situations when true peace wins the battle. This is because the tranquility on the inside, despite the chaos on the outside, eases your mind.

Read Philippians 4:7. How does this passage describe peace?

Have you ever experienced that kind of peace? What were the circumstances?

The Bible says the peace of God is so opposite to the natural way of responding to life's trials that it often comes in a way we can't understand. This is the peace that goes to work for you in spiritual warfare by guarding you from the Enemy's tactics.

God offers us a peace that reaches beyond what we can understand or comprehend. When we receive and walk in that peace, it settles in as a guard over both our hearts and our minds. This is the peace that cradles someone who lost their job so that they don't also lose their mind. This is the peace that produces praise when there is no money in the bank. This is the peace that restores hope in the face of failing health. This is the peace that can come only from the gospel.

Read the following verses:

Romans 1:7
1 Corinthians 1:3
2 Corinthians 1:2
Galatians 1:3
Ephesians 1:2

What do they all have in common?

Paul chose to greet most of his readers in a similar fashion: "Grace and peace to you." Paul was wishing these believers a greater knowledge of the grace of God in Christ and the peace that flows out from that grace.

The gospel tells us that God loves us so much that He sent His Son to die for us (see John 3:16). That's grace. None of us deserve that. Given that God loves us that much, can we really question whether or not He can take care of us in any circumstance? Or that He can actually use any circumstance for our good?

This kind of grace brings peace. And it's the peace that makes sense only to those who understand the gospel, a peace goes peace beyond circumstance.

Pray today about the situations in your life that rob you of peace.
Ask for the peace of God to rain down in your spirit.

## DAY 4

# BEYOND CIRCUMSTANCES

Let's take a look at the kind of peace we've been discussing in action. Perhaps you'll remember the story of three men—Shadrach, Meshach, and Abednego—who exhibited an extraordinary amount of peace, even in the face of tremendous difficulty.

Read Daniel 3:1-7. Based on these verses, what are three words you would use to describe Nebuchadnezzar?

1.

2.

3.

What was so wrong with his actions in this passage?

King Nebuchadnezzar knew how to throw a party—especially if the party was for himself. He certainly had no shortage of ego, for he erected an enormous statue and then called together "people of every nation and language" (v. 4) to fall down and worship his image.

It was a great tribute to a man who, in his own eyes, had gone beyond mere humanity and passed into divinity. On penalty of death, he demanded worship from his kingdom. And that's a problem.

Read Daniel 3:8-18. Based on these verses, what are three words you would use to describe Shadrach, Meshach, and Abednego?

1.

2.

3.

Look at their response to King Nebuchadnezzar in verses 16-18. Where do you see the kind of peace that we're discussing in their statements?

Three men refuse to let some pompous, self-aggrandizing potentate steal the glory that is reserved for God alone. They stand in the midst of a crowd who bows, and that action earns them a one-way trip to the hottest furnace in the land.

The thought of being burned alive in a furnace so hot that it will eventually kill the guards who got close to it (v. 22) definitely qualifies as a peace-robbing circumstance. In the face of such a turn of events, these men would have good reason to be doubtful, fearful, and even angry. Instead, we find an incredible confidence both in the power of God and the wisdom of God. Both are necessary to put on the shoes of the gospel of peace.

Consider those two characteristics: confidence in the power and wisdom of God. Why would embodying those traits enable you to live in peace?

Which do you struggle with more—confidence in God's power or confidence in His wisdom?

Shadrach, Meshach, and Abednego knew that God was more than powerful enough to deliver them from their circumstances. But they were also convinced that God was wise enough to know just how that deliverance should best happen.

Notice that God didn't keep these boys from the fire; they were thrown in. In fact, God allowed the king to light the furnace seven times hotter than normal. In the same way, God often allows us to walk through fires. He doesn't always change our situations and circumstances, though He is more than powerful enough to do so.

Instead of changing their circumstances, God joined Shadrach, Meshach, and Abednego in the fire. The passage tells us that three men were thrown into the furnace, but when the king went to watch them burn, he saw four men, unbound and walking around in the fire.

Is there a situation in your life that God, in His wisdom, has allowed you to walk through that feels like a furnace? Have you sensed God's presence in the furnace with you? How?

When your feet are properly shod, you know God is powerful enough to deliver you. You know He is wise enough to know when and how that deliverance needs to happen. And in the meantime, you know He is with you in the furnace. He will join you in your situation and will give you the peace you need.

Believe in His power. Believe in His wisdom. Believe in His presence. And feel the peace of God that surpasses understanding.

Pray today about a situation in your own life or in the life of a friend that feels like a furnace. Pray that you or your friend will be confident of these attributes of God.

# PUTTING ON THE SHOES

Isaiah gives us the perfect prescription for how to strap on peace shoes: "You will keep the mind that is dependent on You in perfect peace, for it is trusting in You" (26:3). Pay close attention to this principle; it literally has the power to restore all aspects of your life. When your mind agrees with God's mind—His truth and His standard—you will access God's power for victory in spiritual warfare. He will give you your peace shoes.

Trusting God produces peace.

*Trust* is a word Christians are familiar with, but what does it mean? Provide a definition in your own words below.

Is there a particular situation in which you are struggling to trust God right now? Why do you think you are struggling?

Peace from God can't be separated from trust in God. But trust isn't simply a feeling or something you fall in or out of. Trust is active. It's a choice. And it's one you have to make every day—sometimes every hour. When you choose to trust, you are choosing to believe what you know to be true about God rather than what your circumstances might dictate to you.

Often those two things come into conflict. Here's one example. Let's just say you have lost your job. Sure, there is a severance package, but that's quickly running out. Every lead for future employment seems to be a dead end. The phone isn't ringing because you can't get hiring managers to call you back. In the meantime, the bank account is running low. Your family needs to eat, and the mortgage needs to be paid.

Now if you let your circumstances dictate truth, you would be filled with worry and anxiety. Where will the money come from? How will you keep the lights on? These are real questions that would dominate your thinking day in and day out.

But you don't have to believe what your circumstances suggest. Putting on the shoes of peace involves looking past your circumstances to what you know to be true about God.

> Read Romans 5:8; 8:31-32. What themes do you find present in both passages?

> Why is it meaningful that God's love is *proved* at the cross?

God did far more than sit on His throne and yell down from heaven, "I love you! I love you! I love you!" God's love is a proven, demonstrated, and authenticated love. We measure God's love and provision not by our circumstances, but by the historically proven reality of the cross.

As Paul says, if God loved us enough to give up His Son for us, how can we doubt that He will continue to provide for our needs and take care of us (see Rom. 8:32)? When our circumstances cause us to worry and doubt, we beat back those thoughts from the demonic realm by reminding ourselves over and over again of the gospel. We remind ourselves that God's love is no longer in question; it's been proved at the cross.

What are three practical ways you might remind yourself this week
of God's proven love at the cross?

1.


2.


3.


If you've lost your job and don't know how you are going to buy food for your family, don't panic. If you are in the middle of a conflict with your family and can't see how reconciliation will come, don't worry. If you are facing an uncertain future because of a diagnosis, don't fret. Choose to trust, and base your trust in the proven love of God for you.

Meditate on God's Word. Trust in it. Let its truth sink down deep into your heart. Exchange God's promises with the lies that your circumstances bring into your mind. While you are meditating on these truths, exchange your soul's perspective on your situation with what your spirit knows to be true.

Every attack on peace in your life needs to be taken to the spiritual realm and replaced with what God has to say on the matter. When that happens, you will wear shoes unlike any others. These shoes will let the demonic realm, yourself, and others know that you are covered by God's armor. You will walk without becoming weary, and you will find the calming power of peace.

Pray scriptural truth over your life circumstances today. Express
your choice to trust in God and His promises rather than in what
you can see.

1. *Forest Gump,* DVD, directed by Robert Zemeckis (1994; Hollywood, CA: Paramount Pictures, 2001).
2. Harold W. Hoehner, *Ephesians: An Exegetical Commentary* (Grand Rapids, MI: Baker Academic, 2002), 842.
3. Ibid.

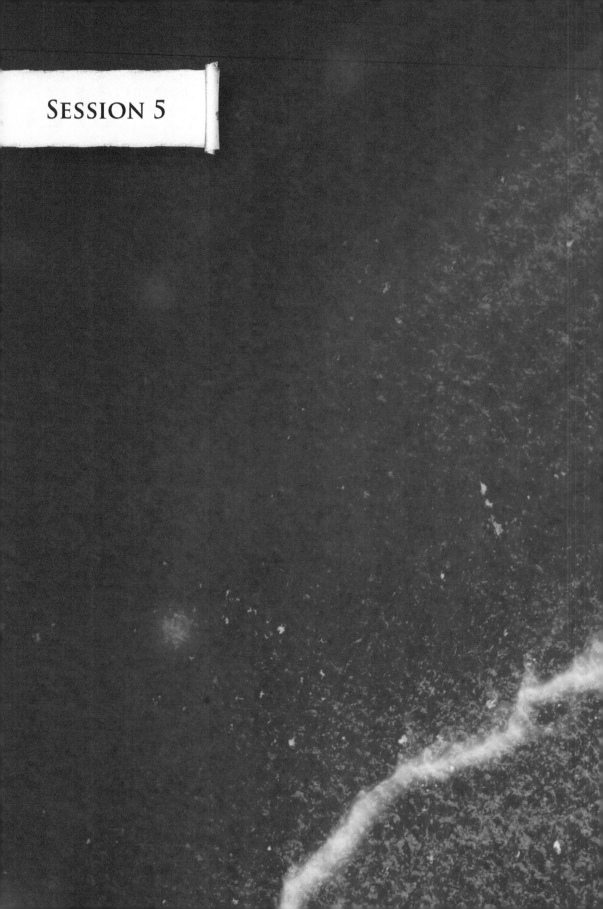

# SESSION 5

SHIELD OF FAITH

## SESSION 5

# THE SHIELD OF FAITH

## GETTING STARTED

1. Share one insight you gained through your personal devotions this week.

2. Did your definition of the gospel expand over the past week? How so?

3. The next piece of armor is the shield of faith. What is the role of faith in the Christian life?

## ARMING UP

**Watch the teaching segment from the DVD using the viewer guide below.**

The shield is actually _____ itself.

The last three pieces of armor are picked up as the _____ demands.

It is your _____ to take up the shield of faith; God won't do it for you.

When positioned correctly, the shield would cover _____ of the Roman soldier.

Faith is _____ on the truth.

Faith is not based on how you _____.

_____ dictate feelings.

When we allow faith to be _____ by feelings, we will always be _____.

Faith is the point of _____ of what God has already done.

Everything God is ever going to do for you He's _____ done.

_____ puts on deposit all of God's goodness on your behalf.

_____ accesses the deposits.

_____ proves you are exhibiting faith.

Real faith cannot be limited to your five _____.

If there is no _____ on what has been prescribed, there is no faith that has been exhibited.

If we will take faith seriously—as God defines it—we will experience _____ as we've never had it before.

**Discuss the teaching with your group, using the questions below.**

1. Why must faith be rooted in the truth rather than how you feel?

2. Is there any area of your life (marriage, parenting, finances, career, or others) in which it is difficult for you to exercise faith? Why?

3. What are some ways your group might encourage each other in faith this week?

**Close with prayer.**

Video sessions available at www.bhpublishinggroup.com/victoryinspiritualwarfare
or with a subscription to smallgroup.com

105

# GET IN THE FIGHT!

"Without faith it is impossible to please God,
for the one who draws near to Him must
believe that he exists and rewards those
who seek Him" Hebrews 11:6

- Read all of Hebrews 11 this week. Journal about the characters you identified with the most.

- Review all your Scripture memory verses from the previous weeks in addition to learning the verse above.

# SESSION FIVE

Perhaps you've seen video of the space shuttle returning to earth. Sure, the runway is longer, but the landing appears to be very similar to that of any other aircraft: it descends at an angle and then touches down and eventually brakes to a halt. But the space shuttle is different.

When it returns to earth after having accomplished its mission, it would never be able to land safely if it were not surrounded by a heat shield. Because of the great altitude and speed at which the shuttle reenters the atmosphere, a tremendous amount of heat is generated on the underside of the craft. During this reentry process, temperatures on the craft reach upwards of three thousand degrees Fahrenheit.

Exposure to that kind of heat would burn up any craft and everyone inside it in just a matter of seconds if it were not completely protected. With a heat shield, flames and smoke can engulf the entire capsule, but nothing on the inside is damaged at all.

*Similarly, taking up the shield of faith enables a believer to live a life of victory in an atmosphere that has the potential to bring harm.*

# DAY 1 | WHAT IS THE SHIELD?

So far we have looked at three pieces in the armor of God that you need to wear in order to be well dressed for warfare. The verb tense used in regard to the first three pieces indicates they should be worn all the time. We are to *have* the belt of truth, *have* the breastplate of righteousness, and *have* the shoes of the gospel of peace.

But at this point in the text, the verb tense changes. The next three pieces are what you are to have at hand, ready to pick up and use when you need them.

> Read Ephesians 6:14-17. Why do you think the first three pieces are to be worn all the time and the next three pieces are meant to be taken up as the situation demands?

> What might that indicate about the difference in nature between the first three pieces and second three?

Think about it in terms of a baseball player who suits up in his uniform for a ball game. He never removes his uniform, but he picks up his bat or his glove as needed. While the bat and the glove are provided by the team and made available to him at all times, it is the ballplayer's responsibility to grab them and use them when he is supposed to. No one forces him to do that, just as God doesn't force the shield of faith, helmet of salvation, or sword of the Spirit into our hands when we need them most. God makes them available to us, instructing us to use them when the situation calls for it.

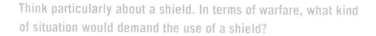

Think particularly about a shield. In terms of warfare, what kind
of situation would demand the use of a shield?

Now think about that in spiritual terms. What kind of spiritual situation
might demand the use of a shield?

Why do you think this shield is linked with faith? In what way might faith
serve as a shield?

A Roman soldier's shield would typically measure 2 ½ feet wide and 4 feet in length.
During battle, it would be situated in such a way that the soldier could crouch
down and hide underneath it when being targeted by arrows.

When positioned correctly underneath the protection of a shield, the soldier would
be completely covered. In fact, soldiers could come together in such a way as to
link their shields next to one another so that the entire army could hide behind
whatever was thrown at them—whether arrows, javelins, or anything else meant to
annihilate and destroy.

The shield could serve, when used correctly, as an impenetrable barrier between its
carrier and the incoming danger.

Look back at Ephesians 6:13. When does the Christian need to take up
the shield?

The "evil day" is the day when all hell breaks loose in your life. It's the day when you are under attack. It's when the finances are so low you don't know how you're going to make it through the end of the week. It's when you've lost your job and there are no openings in sight. It's when you have broken down emotionally and have lost your passion for life. It's when your marriage seems hopeless, your kids have turned away, your health deteriorates, your future looks bleak, or you are overcome by an addiction or impulse.

Do any of the previous examples resemble your current situation?

How could having the shield of faith in your hands serve you in this particular situation?

It is on this evil day that you need to be covered more than ever. You need a shield. You need protection because this is the day when you are most vulnerable, tired, and exposed to the targeted attacks of the Evil One.

Rest assured, the attacks of the Evil One are indeed targeted. Satan doesn't blindly fire his arrows into the air, hoping one of them will strike. He knows you. He knows your deepest fears, insecurities, and tendencies. That's where the arrows are aimed. They are personal arrows, targeted toward the most vulnerable areas of your life.

Maybe you're feeling targeted right now. He's hitting you where it counts—where it really hurts. The days are evil, and because they are, there is no better time to pick up the piece of protective armor that is at your disposal right now.

Pray today that you will stand firm in faith against the targeted attacks of the Evil One.

## DAY 2 | FAITH IS ...

The shield is actually faith itself. So in order to know what it is we are to shield ourselves behind, we need to fully understand both the content and the scope of faith. Faith is critical to achieving victory in spiritual warfare.

Define *faith*.

Read Hebrews 11:1. How does your definition fit with the one in this verse?

The most simple and direct definition I can give you of *faith* is *believing God is telling the truth*. Another way of saying it is that faith is believing something is a certain way, just because God said so, even when it appears to be otherwise.

For example, let's say your marriage is struggling. You and your spouse are both under spiritual attack. There are financial struggles and temptations of infidelity. But you know God's revealed truth is that infidelity and divorce must be replaced by strong communication and sacrificial love. You believe that to be true, even though you can't see how that will help your marriage. That is faith.

So, you see, there is a strong link between faith and truth.

In your own words, how is faith related to God's revealed truth?

It's no surprise that the belt of truth was the first piece of armor listed, because many of the other pieces are interconnected with truth in some way. If you don't know the truth or if you don't act on the truth, the shield of faith is impotent. In order to have faith, you must know and respond to truth. And as we saw earlier, truth is fundamentally God's viewpoint on a matter.

Faith is only as valuable as the thing to which it is connected. Think about it like this. You're standing in a room with no furniture, and you want to sit down. You look around and see there is no chair, but you close your eyes and believe as hard as you can that there is a chair underneath you. Then you take a deep breath and sit.

What happens? You're pulling yourself up off the ground with a bruised tailbone. You can believe as long and as hard as you want, but faith is only as good as the thing to which it is connected.

What kinds of things, other than the God revealed in Scripture, might people connect their faith to?

What about you? What is your faith currently connected to? How do you know?

Faith involves knowing the God who has revealed Himself in the Bible. You choose to believe in His revealed truth, even if that truth doesn't seem to match your experience. That's the intellectual component of faith. But faith is more than knowing a set of facts and believing them to be true.

Faith also involves action.

Scan Hebrews 11. For each verse below, record the character mentioned and their actions.

| Verse | Character | Actions |
|-------|-----------|---------|
| 11:4  |           |         |
| 11:7  |           |         |
| 11:8  |           |         |
| 11:11 |           |         |
| 11:17 |           |         |
| 11:24 |           |         |

Get the point? It's not enough to intellectually acknowledge certain things to be true. Through the lives of these men and women, faith showed up in their feet. None of these individuals simply said they believed in God and what He has promised. Instead, we read that each one responded in faith, as is revealed in their actions.

By faith each one reached down and picked up the shield instead of letting it lean against the wall. What would happen to a Roman soldier if he said he believed his shield would protect him, but he never grabbed it? He would be dead as quickly as an arrow could be shot through his throat.

Do you believe God wants to save your marriage? Start serving your spouse. Do you believe God will provide your family with income? Keep looking for a job—any job. Do you believe God wants your children to know Him? Keep telling them about Jesus. Faith is believing so strongly in God's revealed truth that it shows up in the way you live your life. Faith is about the mind and the feet: intellect and action.

Pray today that you will link your mind and your feet together in your practice of faith.

## DAY 3 | FAITH IS NOT ...

Sometimes we don't *feel* like believing. That's because believing is often difficult. Paul said the days are evil. And it's during those times of difficulty that we simply don't feel God's presence. We, therefore, don't feel like believing.

But faith is acting on the truth whether or not I feel the truth. It's acting on the truth whether or not I like the truth. It's acting on the truth whether or not I agree with the truth. Faith is a function of the mind that shows up in the feet.

Notice that nowhere in the previous paragraph do we act according to our feelings. That is very important to recognize.

Can you trust your feelings in most situations? Why or why not?

Recall one situation below when you found that your feelings were untrustworthy.

When we allow our faith to be defined by our feelings, we'll only end up confused. Faith must have an objective standard by which it is defined—truth. In fact, when faith operates by an objective standard of truth, it will eventually dictate our emotions.

Did you get that? Truth dictates emotions. Not the other way around. Often we do the thing God has asked us to do without the accompanying emotions to go with it. However, as you continue to walk by faith in the direction God has called you, your emotions soon follow.

As an example, read Matthew 5:43-48. In reading this passage, where do you see Jesus recognizing the emotional difficulty in loving your enemies?

Even the tax collectors love those who love them. But it takes someone different to love a perceived enemy. Loving someone who has betrayed you, hurt you, gossiped about you, or disgraced you is difficult, and you probably won't feel like doing so. But if, by faith, you choose to do good to someone you perceive to be an enemy, one day the emotion of love will override the emotions of hate, anger, or bitterness you feel.

By faith you are trusting that someday you will feel the way you are supposed to feel. You act accordingly. Luke 5 provides a powerful illustration of this principle at work.

Read Luke 5:1-11. What did Peter feel in this passage?

How did he exercise faith that looked beyond his feelings?

I can actually hear the sigh in Peter's words as he carefully tries to answer Jesus after Jesus commanded him to "put out into deep water and let down your nets for a catch" (v. 4).

"Master," he says, in my Tony Evans translation, "You stick with preaching. You're good at it. But I've been fishing all my life, as far back as I can remember. In fact, these boats are part of the Zebedee Corporation. We've even got a fancy logo. And beyond that, just so you are clear, we've been fishing for 12 hours straight. The fish aren't biting. And if they're not biting at night, they're sure not going to be biting during the day.

Furthermore, if you knew anything about fishing, you'd know we're in shallow water right now, which is definitely not the place to catch fish. Throwing down our nets now is not only ridiculous but also a waste of time and energy."

Peter clearly didn't feel like doing what Jesus said to do, but he did it anyway. It made no sense, it required great effort, and it forced Peter to turn his back on logic—but he did it. And as the boat was sinking under the weight of all the fish they were never supposed to catch, I wonder whether Jesus grinned a little at Peter.

Think of a situation in your life in which you don't feel like acting according to God's truth. Consider if any of the following might fit. Then describe what God's revealed truth says to do in that situation:

Marriage:

Relationship with coworker or boss:

Parent:

Friend:

Peter discovered that day that faith is acting on what God says in spite of your own knowledge, background, experience, education, and especially feelings. Faith begins by knowing truth and then acting on truth so that you can see God move, even if you don't feel like it.

Pray through the situation you described above. Ask for the courage it will take to act according to God's revealed truth on the matter.

## DAY 4    ARROWS

Imagine you are a Roman soldier preparing for battle. You begin to put on your armor—the belt, the breastplate, and the shoes. Then you go and pick up your shield; it's long and strong, and just holding it gives you a feeling of safety and protection. You turn to your right and see one of your fellow soldiers doing something to his shield.

As you watch, he wraps his shield in leather or another kind of animal skin. Then he systematically begins to plunge it into a vat of water over and over again until it's dripping wet. The point of such an action is obvious: a wet shield would instantly snuff out a fiery arrow that was fired.

Similarly, Paul warns that Satan is going to shoot fiery arrows your way. These kinds of arrows are meant to burn up your defenses so that you will then be vulnerable to other kinds of attacks he's going to send your way. But the shield of faith is there not only to protect you from the attack but also to put out the fire meant to expose you.

> Read 1 John 5:4-5. According to this passage, what is the victory that has conquered the world?

> What, stated in verse 5, is this faith linked to?

Faith is so powerful that this passage declares it to be the key to victory in whatever we face in the world. This key is rooted in the cross because there Jesus Christ accomplished the ultimate victory.

Read Jesus' final words on the cross in John 19:30. What do you think Jesus meant when He said, "It is finished"?

How might that phrase have relevance in our battle against spiritual darkness?

From Jesus' own mouth we find the declaration of the ultimate victory. On the cross all the sin of the world—past, present, and future—was nailed to Him. If Jesus was able to not only overcome the destruction of those sins but was also raised up in victory over them, He is more than able to overcome any destructive force you are facing right now in spiritual warfare.

It would be like asking a weightlifter who regularly bench-presses 500 pounds if he is going to have a problem carrying a bag of groceries into the house from the car. If he can handle the 500 pounds, he can handle your groceries.

If Jesus Christ could handle and overcome all the sin of the world on the cross, do we really think our situation is too difficult for Him to handle? What about our marriage? Our employment? Our relational difficulties? The good news is that God—not you—is responsible for upholding your faith.

Read Philippians 1:6 and Hebrews 12:2. Combine those two verses together in a statement below about God's role in our faith.

If you really believed God is the initiator, upholder, and finisher of your faith, how might it change your understanding of your ability to take up the shield?

Often the shield of faith feels very heavy. We find ourselves beaten down by the attacks of the Enemy. We are tired—spiritually, emotionally, and physically. It's during those moments that we have the opportunity to ask ourselves where our faith is truly directed. Are we trusting in our own ability to have faith, or are we trusting that God is powerful enough to keep us in the faith?

Why is making a distinction between those two questions important?

Which are you trusting in right now: your ability to have faith or God's ability to uphold your faith?

Read Isaiah 40:28-31. What promises do you find in this passage that relate to God's ability to uphold us?

When we look past our own failing strength, we will actually find our strength renewed. Jesus has already won the ultimate victory on the cross, and because He did, we know God is never going to leave us in the battle by ourselves.

Even now, if you listen closely, you can hear the voice of the Lord reminding you: "Trust in me. Don't trust in yourself. I have begun a good work in you, and I will carry it to completion. Now, with my strength, reach down and grab that shield."

When we do that, we are beginning to understand how to take up the shield God has given to us for protection.

Pray today, confessing your own weakness but also acknowledging God's strength. Take your eyes off your own ability and place them on the strength of Christ within you.

# TAKING UP THE SHIELD

God is the Beginner of our faith. He is the Upholder of our faith. He is the Finisher of our faith. He will carry us all the way to completion. That truth is the basis of how we take up the shield.

We need to understand that faith doesn't make God move. All faith does is access what God has already done. If you think faith makes God move, you're going to be searching for a way to get more faith. However, as a Christian, you already have all the faith you need to access anything God is going to do for you.

Read Luke 17:5-6. Have you ever asked God to increase your faith? What were the circumstances?

What was Jesus' point in His response?

Is this passage encouraging or discouraging to you? Why?

As the saying goes, "A little dab will do ya." You don't need more faith. You need to know more truth. This is because faith is the point of access, not the point of power. The power is in what God has already declared and completed in grace when he deposited the divine life within you in seed form.

But there's a funny thing about seeds: they grow. As you tend them with water and sunlight, something that began as small as a mustard seed grows and grows and grows. Likewise, as you feed the seed of faith within you with attention to God's truth and His presence, it expands and grows, offering you access to all God has in store for you. The role of faith is to draw upon what grace has already put on deposit.

That growth takes many different forms. It's the growing of virtues like love and patience. It's the formation of spiritual habits and disciplines. It's the denial of temptation and self. And the seed continues to grow, all because we access it by faith.

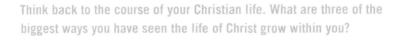

Think back to the course of your Christian life. What are three of the biggest ways you have seen the life of Christ grow within you?

1.


2.


3.


Get this straight: faith is the access point for victory. Not works. Often we believe works are what we need to do to access what God has in store for us in His grace. That is, we think that in order to obtain victory, we need to work harder. We need to go to church more. Read the Bible more. Give more. Be nicer people.

Those aren't bad things, but they won't result in victorious living. In fact, those things, done apart from faith, really have very little value at all. Works, when done correctly, flow from faith. They prove the existence of faith. But they can never supplant faith.

Read John 6:28-29. What, according to Jesus, are the "works of God"?

Is His answer surprising to you? Why or why not?

The people came to Jesus with a simple question. They asked what, specifically, God required them to do. Jesus' reply is interesting. He told them the work they need to *do* is to *believe*.

He would say the same thing to us. Habakkuk 2:4 says, "The righteous will live by his faith." To live by faith means that faith becomes the regular way of thinking, doing, and being. This is the kind of faith that shows up in the way you walk, move, talk, and make decisions. Living by faith means faith becomes your groove—it's your zone. It's what the Bible calls walking by faith.

That means you take an entirely different perspective on every situation in your life. You choose to view that situation through the lens of faith rather than your physical eyes. Many times those two views won't line up, but that's the nature of faith. By definition, faith is in the realm of the unseen.

Today the question isn't so much what you will do but rather what you will believe. What will you believe about your finances? About your addiction? About your temptation? About your loneliness? Will you use your faith to access the grace inside and act accordingly?

If you will, then you've picked up the shield. And you'll be safe behind it.

Pray today for the ability to look at your life through the lens of faith.

# SESSION 6

# HELMET OF SALVATION

# SESSION 6

# THE HELMET OF SALVATION

## GETTING STARTED

1. Share one insight you gained through your personal devotions this week.

2. Share one instance this past week when you chose to exercise faith. What were the results?

3. The next piece of armor is the helmet of salvation. Why might salvation be linked to a piece of armor that protects the head?

## ARMING UP

**Watch the teaching segment from the DVD using the viewer guide below.**

The _____ must be protected to absorb the shocks of being hit in the spiritual realm by the Enemy.

"Putting on the helmet" means to _____ the mind.

The only way you can consistently change your _____ is to change your _____.

Without proper _____, there will be faulty life.

The helmet is a helmet called _____.

Salvation is by _____, through faith, unto good _____.

The same way you got saved is the same way you _____ as saved.

Grace is _____ that God has done for you independent of you.

You _____ grace by the means of faith.

The moment you try to access grace by _____, you nullify grace.

Faith is my _____ _____ to what God has already done.

"saved"—to be _____

_____ is injected into sin.

You get rid of the _____ by having the power to deal with the sin.

**Discuss the teaching with your group, using the questions below.**

1. Why is it important to see that salvation is by grace, through faith, and unto good works?

2. Which part of that definition of faith do you think is most neglected by Christians?

3. How does our outlook on life change when we see that we are to live in the same way that we have been saved?

**Close with prayer.**

Video sessions available at www.bhpublishinggroup.com/victoryinspiritualwarfare
or with a subscription to smallgroup.com

127

# GET IN THE FIGHT!

"You are saved by grace through faith, and
this is not from yourselves; it is God's gift—
not from works, so that no one can boast.
For we are His creation, created in Christ Jesus
for good works, which God prepared ahead
of time so that we should walk in them."
Ephesians 2:8-10

Guard your mind this week by writing down every television show or movie you watch. Are these influences serving to build your mind for good works? If not, talk with a spouse or friend about how your daily patterns might change.

Since salvation is for good works, ask God to show you this week what good works He has planned for you. Make this a daily prayer and then take advantage of the opportunities before you.

# SESSION SIX

A man who owned a tattoo parlor was once asked, "Why do you think so many people come in here to get tattoos?"

The shop owner replied without any hesitation: "Because before there is ever a tattoo on the body, there is a tattoo on the mind."

In other words, people merely display on their bodies what has already been displayed in their minds. The mind is incredibly powerful. What a person thinks often shows up in their five senses. What begins as a thought eventually manifests itself as something we can see, touch, taste, hear, or smell.

To a degree, what we receive and process in our minds will eventually control our actions. That can be either incredibly positive and uplifting or incredibly negative and destructive.

*Perhaps that's why the next piece of armor we need to take up in this battle of spiritual warfare is a helmet.*

# DAY 1

# WHAT IS THE HELMET?

The main purpose of a helmet—in battle, sports, or even risky situations like construction—is to protect the head from injury to the brain. A football player's helmet is padded on the inside to help absorb shock when the player gets pounded to the ground. The brain must be protected at all costs, because once the brain becomes damaged, body function is impaired. A football player suffering from the ongoing effects of too many concussions can no longer play at the physical level he once could. In fact, he may not even be able to play, or function, at all.

Why do you think the helmet is linked with salvation?

Why must the mind be protected in spiritual warfare?

With the helmet, Paul once again uses a physical example to illustrate a spiritual truth. This is because the brain is to the body what the mind is to the soul. It's the control center for the functioning of the will and emotions. In the spiritual realm, the mind must be protected with a helmet that is able to absorb the shocks of being hit and knocked to the ground by the Enemy.

When our minds no longer function as they were designed to, the mind impedes both our will and emotions from doing what they are supposed to do. Since this is so, one of Satan's primary strategies is to attack our minds. In fact, it is such a critical area that we see the theme of the mind occurring in each of the different pieces of armor we are to wear in warfare.

Think back over the course of your study so far. Where do you recall seeing the mind come up in regard to the other pieces of the armor?

What are some ways you sense that Satan has attacked your mind as a Christian?

Read the following passages of Scripture. For each one, note the action prescribed in regard to your mind.

Psalm 26:2-3

Isaiah 26:2-4

Mark 12:30

Romans 8:5-6

Romans 12:1-2

The mind is imperative for spiritual victory. We are to guard our minds, renew our minds, ask God to search our minds, and love God with our minds. Often we think about spiritual victory occurring in our actions—that we say no to temptation, addiction, or frustration. But any victory manifested in the physical actions has first been won inside our own heads.

Conversely, spiritual defeat begins with a tiny, insignificant thought in the mind that eventually grows into depraved action.

Look at this process in action in Romans 1:18-25. Record below all the references to the mind or thinking from these verses.

In your own words, what is the progression of sin from mind to body in this passage?

We can know something about God just from looking at the greatness of nature. However, we often choose to replace that knowledge in our minds with evil thoughts. We've kept those thoughts in our heads so long that our entire way of thinking has become nonsense. We're upside down and twisted up in our heads. That way of thinking eventually comes out in the form of things like sexual impurity and idol worship.

What we have in our minds becomes our grid for reality and truth. If the mind, the spiritual expression of the brain, operates on a false grid of reality and truth, then the body will also function according to that false reality. In other words, if a person's perspective is errant and the mind-set is flawed, then that person's function will also be flawed.

Take some time for a thought evaluation. What do you spend the bulk of your time thinking, fantasizing, or dreaming about? Money? Sex? Power?

Now think critically about your actions. How has dwelling on those kinds of things changed your behavior?

Satan knows that if he can keep us from wearing the helmet of salvation to protect our minds, he can whisper his own version of truth into our ears. When our minds are unprotected, we will eventually begin to believe the lies we hear from him and act accordingly.

But to wear the helmet well, we've got to understand a bit more about salvation.

Pray today, confessing the things you listed above that occupy your thought life. Then spend time dwelling on God's revealed truth instead of the lies of the Enemy.

# DAY 2 | SALVATION THEN

When a soldier goes into battle, any old helmet won't do. Paul knew that when he wrote about the weapons of warfare. That's why he specifically said to take up the helmet of *salvation*. But what is interesting to note about Paul's use of the word *salvation* is that he was writing to people who were already saved.

The Book of Ephesians was written to people whom Paul refers to as "saints," "the faithful," and those who have already been blessed "in Christ with every spiritual blessing in the heavens" (Eph. 1:1,3). The implication is that a Christian can be an "unsaved saved" person, because Paul is telling believers to pick up and put on the helmet of salvation.

At the core of most of our problems, and we all have them to varying degrees and at different levels, is our lack of understanding of salvation.

Define *salvation*.

Briefly describe your own salvation experience below.

Do you think you have a full understanding of salvation? Why or why not?

Write down a few questions you have about the nature, scope, or process of salvation below.

1.

2.

3.

Heaven and hell. That's what salvation is about to most people. We once were bound for hell, but when we were saved, we got a new ticket with "heaven" stamped as the final destination point. That's true enough, but it's not the only implication of salvation.

Salvation is not exclusively about the future; salvation has profound implications for your life and spiritual victory right now. A good beginning point to see this is through the way Jesus described salvation.

Let me set the scene for you. Jesus and His buddies are lounging around in a room. There is a knock at the door, and a hooded figure stands at the threshold. It's the last person any of the boys expected to see that night—Nicodemus, a Pharisee who only hours earlier had been among the other Pharisees leveling insults at Jesus. But this encounter is different.

Nicodemus has come because he needs some answers.

Read the rest of this account for yourself in John 3:1-3. According to Jesus, what must happen to a person in order to see the kingdom of God?

Why do you think Jesus chose this particular phrase to describe salvation?

Nicodemus was understandably confused. How could a person be born again? Does that mean he gets back into his mother's womb? Jesus corrects the Pharisee's thinking by informing him that He's referring to a spiritual birth. Salvation is such a dramatic and radical change that the only way to describe it is to compare it to being born a second time.

When a person trusts in Christ for the forgiveness of their sins, an instantaneous change occurs. This change is called justification. Justification is the removal of the *penalty* of sin, along with a declaration of legal righteousness.

This change is immediate, whether or not we recognize it. Paul would later describe justification in his letter to the church at Corinth.

Read 2 Corinthians 5:17-21. Notice the verb tenses in this passage. What do the past tense verbs refer to?

The old is gone. The new is here. That's what happens at justification. Justification is salvation in the past tense for any believer. It's irrevocable and sealed. We have been saved, and that gives us an enormous amount of security in moving forward. No matter what the Enemy might tell you, you can always remind yourself of the past tense of justification. God did it, and no one or nothing can ever take it away from you.

However, it's equally important to note that while salvation refers to justification and the implanting of the new life in the form of an imperishable seed within our spirit, it does not refer *only* to that. Salvation is an all-inclusive word that summarizes all Christ has provided for us—past, present, and future.

Spend time in prayer today thanking God for justifying you. Then ask Him to open your eyes to see the fullness of salvation in the present and future tenses.

SALVATION NOW

We have been justified. Every Christian can say that—it's past tense. It is through justification that the *penalty* of sin is removed. But justification is just the beginning of the entire scope of salvation.

The present tense of the word *salvation* is the ongoing renewal of a person through the work of the indwelling Holy Spirit. This removes the *power* of sin over a believer and is called sanctification. Glorification, the future tense of salvation, is the removal of the presence of sin. Thus, when the Bible speaks about salvation, it can be referring to justification, sanctification, or glorification.

When you think of salvation, are you more prone to think about it in past, present, or future terms? Why?

Why do you think it's important to have a holistic view of salvation?

Read James 1:21. Is this verse referring to the past, present, or future focus of salvation? How do you know?

What is "the implanted word, which is able to save you"?

Sanctification is our focus as we look at the helmet of salvation. James wrote this verse to fellow believers, just as Paul did with the Ephesians, who were already saved in the sense of justification. He urged his listeners to continue to humbly receive the gospel—the implanted word—which is able to save them. Salvation in this passage is the process of one becoming more like Christ.

> Paul used the same meaning of *salvation* when he wrote Romans 1:16. Read this verse. Fill in the blanks below.
>
> The gospel is _____ _____ for _____.

The use of the word *salvation* in this verse means *to be delivered*. It is the power of God to deliver not only from hell in the future but also from hell in the present.

There are a number of things that God needs to deliver you from in your daily life. It could be an addiction, a wrong relationship, an unhealthy mind-set, a stronghold, or emotional bondage. The Enemy knows that all he has to do is push the right button to make you think something you shouldn't. But the gospel has the power to deliver you from that.

In order to see that deliverance, we must once again understand that salvation is not only a past moment. Nor is it only a future destiny. Salvation is *right now*.

> Look at another example of the multidimensional nature of salvation in Ephesians 2:8-10. Complete the following statements below based on this passage.
>
> Salvation is by _____.
>
> Salvation is through _____.
>
> Salvation is for _____ _____.

All of these components make up the package that we call salvation—salvation that is by grace, through faith, and for good works. Paul's letter to the church in Colossae emphasizes this truth when he writes, "As you have received Christ Jesus the Lord, walk in Him" (Col. 2:6). Paul is telling the believers in Colossae that the same way they were saved—by grace, through faith, and for good works—is the same way they are to function as they are being saved. Recognizing this critical truth is essential to living a life of victory because it emphasizes the holistic nature of the gospel.

Which of those components of salvation—that it's by grace, through faith, and for good works—is most difficult for you to accept? Why?

Why is it important to have a balance between those three components in your understanding of salvation? What might someone's perspective look like if they got out of balance?

Let's say you love to think about salvation by grace, but you never think about it as being for good works. You're likely to become lazy, simply sitting around waiting to die and go to heaven without any regard for the battle going on around you. On the other hand, if you overemphasize salvation for good works, you're apt to lapse into legalism, trying to earn God's approval, which has already been given to you through Jesus.

When we keep these three aspects of salvation in tension, we will live in spiritual victory. We will know that our minds are protected by the helmet of salvation, because we will start to understand the fullness of what salvation really is.

Pray today about the aspect of salvation you tend to underemphasize (as you have previously noted). Pray for balance in your understanding of these three elements.

# DAY 4 | GRACE, FAITH, GOOD WORKS

Unless we understand that salvation is by grace, through faith, and for good works—the way God defines it—we will be grabbing any old hat and trying it on for size and attempting to pass it off as a helmet.

In the meantime, our skull will get cracked by the Enemy. I don't know about you, but if I'm in a battle, I don't want a ball cap on my head. I want something strong and hard. I want a helmet. So let's consider those three components a little further and see how they rightly relate to one another.

Define *grace.*

Do you have a hard time accepting grace? Why or why not?

Grace is all about what God has done for you, independently of you. You have no responsibility in grace being grace. This is part of the reason we surprisingly have trouble with the notion of grace.

Most every other relationship we are in, to some degree, is based on performance. You quit performing at work, and you get fired. You start treating your friends badly, and you'll get dropped. You stop paying your mortgage, and you get foreclosed. We have been conditioned to believe that our acceptance is based on our performance.

But grace is unmerited favor. It's blessing completely independent of our performance. And it goes beyond our wildest measurements and expectations. Every opportunity God is ever going to open up for you has already been opened. Every stronghold He is ever going to break in you has already been broken. The joy you are looking for already exists. The peace you are praying for is already present. Even the power you need to live the life God has created you to live, you already have.

Read Paul's affirmation of these truths in Ephesians 1:3. Do you have trouble believing these things to be true? Why or why not?

If this is true, then why aren't more of the previously mentioned things actualized?

The answer to this question is not about the lack of what you already have. The answer is about how you access what you already have by grace. This is where faith comes into the picture. You access what's been given to you by grace through faith, and through faith alone.

What we often try to do is access our spiritual blessings that have been given to us by grace through good works. In a sense, we try to bargain with God; "I will give You my good works in exchange for Your spiritual blessings."

Have you ever tried to strike a bargain with God? When?

What is wrong with doing so?

We try to bargain with good things—church attendance, giving away money, treating our neighbors nicely, and on and on. Entire theological systems are built on this type of bartering, that God is willing to exchange greater blessings when we start doing good things for Him.

The problem is not with the good things—they are indeed good things to do. The problem is the motivation behind them. If you are doing good works to try and earn God's favor so that you can access His grace, then you have disqualified yourself from grace simply because your actions have shown that you don't believe in what grace truly is. This type of religion will ultimately defeat you. It will keep you in a posture of trying to earn what has already been freely given.

We have faith in God's work of grace. The good works we do must flow from that grace. We must no longer view good works as a means to earn His favor or to reduce His wrath. It's a subtle difference in the physical realm, but it makes all the difference in the spiritual realm.

Taking up the helmet of salvation involves grace, faith, and good works but only in their proper order and in their proper relationship to one another.

God has given us grace in Christ. Faith is the means by which we access grace. That grace flows into good works. This progression leads us to a simple but essential element in understanding salvation.

In prayer realign your understanding of the progression described. By faith, begin to access the grace God has stored up for you in the heavenlies.

# PUTTING ON
# THE HELMET

Friend, can I let you in on a secret I have discovered from all of my years of ministry and counseling that only few people really know?

God loves you.

In fact, he demonstrated it. God cannot love you any more than He does right now, and the proof is in the death of Jesus Christ. When God sacrificed His own Son and turned His back on Him at the point of His death, He gave you all of the love He could ever give. You don't need to try and make God love you more, because you simply can't.

> Do you agree that few people really understand that God loves them? If so, why do you think that is?

> Think of someone you know who you believe truly understands the love of God. What are three words that characterize their life?
>
> 1.
>
> 2.
>
> 3.

When we try to use good works to access God's grace, we prove that we don't really believe in His already given and proven love for us. We become like children trying to earn our parent's affection. A parent in a healthy and functioning home, set up the way God designed it, already loves that child unconditionally, regardless of what they do or don't do. Children are loved by virtue of their relationship to the one whose love they are trying to gain.

The parent may love the child unconditionally, but it's up to the child to actually believe that to be true. God greatly desires for us to be absolutely convinced of His love for us.

> Read Romans 8:15-16. According to this passage, why has God given us the Holy Spirit?

> Do you typically think of the Spirit in those terms? Why or why not?

God is so concerned that we fully believe in His unconditional Love, that He has given us the Holy Spirit to remind us that we are His children. While we might think the voice of the Holy Spirit is condemning, constantly telling us all the things we do wrong, Paul says the opposite is the case. The Spirit's job is to remind us, over and over again, that we are the beloved children of God.

When you fully embrace that there is nothing you can do to get God to love you more because He's already given you all the love He can possibly give, you will discover the power to live a life of victory. When that truth takes root deep within you, you will have confidence like never before to overcome strongholds and resist temptations. You begin to actually become a whole new you.

> Look again at 2 Corinthians 5:21. How does this passage describe a Christian?

> Do you believe you are the righteousness of God? Why or why not?

It's amazing how far-reaching and yet shortsighted our faith can be. We believe the universe was created from absolutely nothing. We believe Jesus was able to feed thousands with a few morsels. We believe the dead can live and the blind can see. But we so often fail to believe what the Bible says about us.

Look back at some of the ways Paul greeted Christians in his letters. Record the name he uses in each instance below.

Romans 1:7

1 Corinthians 1:2

2 Corinthians 1:1

Ephesians 1:1

Would you call yourself a saint? Why or why not?

Regardless of what you think about yourself, God calls you a saint. A saint is one who is called out—a chosen one. This is how God sees us. Once we are saved, we are made righteous and have a place at God's table alongside Jesus Christ. Do you want to put on the helmet of salvation?

Believe what the Bible says about you!

When you do, you will begin to understand that saying no to temptation, conquering addictions, and breaking down strongholds is the most natural thing in the world. You are accessing, by faith, the power of God that He has already given to you by His grace, and you're applying it to individual areas of life in the form of good works.

That's what saints do. That's who you are. Wearing the helmet of salvation means you believe in what God has done in you, and you act accordingly.

Pray today for the faith to believe what the Bible says to be true about you.

# SESSION 7

# SWORD OF THE SPIRIT

## SESSION 7

# THE SWORD
# OF THE SPIRIT

## GETTING STARTED

1. Share one insight you gained through your personal devotions this week.

2. Did your perspective on your daily life and interactions change as you dwelt this week on the fullness of salvation? How so?

3. The final piece of armor is the sword of the Spirit, the Word of God. Why do you think this is the only offensive weapon in the armor?

## ARMING UP

**Watch the teaching segment from the DVD using the viewer guide below.**

"take"—pick up as _____

The sword of the Spirit is the only _____ weapon in the arsenal.

The sword is a _____, used for up close combat.

The sword is the _____ tool the Spirit uses.

God doesn't need _____ methodology to fight a _____ battle.

The sword is the _____ of God.

graphe—the _____

logos—the _____ of the writings

rhema—_____

The *rhema* is the _____ of the *logos* that you got from
the *graphe*.

The *logos* not only attacks what you _____ but also what you _____.

The goal of the *logos* is to _____.

The spoken word had _____ in it to produce what the spoken word
called for.

If the living Word needed to _____ the written Word to deal with the
Enemy of the Word, how much more must you and I need to do the same?

The issue is not whether your need is _____; the issue is who
is giving you the advice of how to address it.

You _____ the *graphe* so you can _____ the *logos* so you
can _____ the *rhema*.

**Discuss the teaching with your group, using the questions below.**

1. Why is it important to understand the progression from *graphe* to *logos*
   to *rhema*?

2. What happens to your ability to take up this sword if you stop at *graphe*?
   What about if you stop at *logos*?

3. What is one practice you might incorporate into your life this week
   in order to more consistently take up the sword of the Spirit?

**Close with prayer.**

Video sessions available at www.bhpublishinggroup.com/victoryinspiritualwarfare
or with a subscription to smallgroup.com

149

# GET IN THE FIGHT!

"The word of God is living and effective
and sharper than any double-edged sword,
penetrating as far as the separation of soul and
spirit, joints and marrow. it is able to judge the
ideas and thoughts of the heart." Hebrews 4:12

- Download a plan to read the Bible through in one year from www.readthebibleforlife.com.

- Set up a Scripture memory accountability group with people from your Bible study group or other friends to continue the practice of memorizing the Bible after this study.

# SESSION SEVEN

One day an elderly man walked into a local lumberyard and told the owner of the company that he wanted to come and work for him chopping down trees. The owner took one look at the wrinkled old man and laughed. "You're as old as dirt," he said. "What makes you think you have what it takes to work for me?"

"Just give me a chance," the old man replied. "I know I can do this job."

The owner was in a pleasant mood, so he decided to humor the old man by taking him out to the forest where a number of younger men were working. In a matter of hours, to everyone's surprise, the old man had chopped down more trees than any of the younger men. The owner's mouth fell open in amazement. He asked him, "Sir, where did you learn to cut trees like that?"

The old man replied, "You ever heard of the Sahara Forest?"

"You mean the Sahara Desert?" asked the owner.

"No," the old man said, "I mean the Sahara Forest. That's what they called it before I got there."

The final piece of armor is the one we take up to go on the offensive. It's the one we use to wage war with the Enemy. And it's the one, regardless of your age or apparent weakness, that is capable of doing more than you will ever need.

*Time to pick up your sword.*

# DAY 1 | WHAT IS THE SWORD?

We've now come to our final piece in the armor of God. When you successfully put on, take up, and function with all six pieces of the armor, you will have all you need to experience true and lasting victory in spiritual warfare.

> Read Ephesians 6:17. What is unique about this particular piece of armor?

> How would taking up a sword in a physical battle complete your readiness for conflict?

This is the only piece in the arsenal that's an offensive weapon. Everything else is designed to hold you steady from what the Enemy seeks to bring against you in the evil day. But after God has outfitted you for battle in order to stand firm, He now tells you that He is giving you an additional weapon with which you can attack and advance.

> How does your mind-set change when you are given a weapon with which to attack rather than just defend?

The Roman soldier had two very different types of swords that he used in battle. The first sword he carried was called a *spatha*. The spatha was a longer sword, generally about 3 feet in length. The shorter sword, called the *gladius*, typically contained a blade around 24 inches in length.[1] Paul was specific when he told us to take up the sword of the Spirit, designating one of these as the offensive weapon in the battle.

Which sword do you think Paul was referring to? Why?

When Paul instructs us to "take up the sword," the Greek term he uses is *macaira,* which refers to the shorter sword—the gladius.[2]

What are ways a sword like this would be useful in battle?

What implications does that have for the manner of the spiritual battle?

The first image I want you to remove from your mind when you consider this sword is that of Zorro or other swashbucklers in the movies. The gladius, similar to a dagger, was used for up-close, in-your-face type of fighting. The soldier would draw this sword when he found himself in hand-to-hand combat, most often with a solitary opponent. He could use the gladius to deliver an unexpected yet deadly blow to his enemy because the enemy would not see it coming.

The gladius was double-edged on the blade and had a needle-sharp point, allowing for a greater amount of damage at a quicker rate. Oftentimes, a longer sword simply created a wound that might have been painful but would not have disabled the opponent. But the gladius delivered a deathblow straight to the core of the opponent, either in his heart or in his midsection. A 2-inch gouge from a dagger often proved to be fatal more quickly than any length of a swipe from a longer sword.

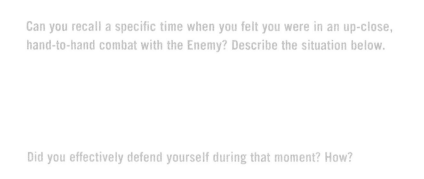

Can you recall a specific time when you felt you were in an up-close, hand-to-hand combat with the Enemy? Describe the situation below.

Did you effectively defend yourself during that moment? How?

What about going on the offensive? Were you able to do that?

When Paul instructs us to take up the sword of the Spirit, he is also letting us know that sometimes in this battle the Enemy is so close that it seems as if he is right there in your face. In fact, it can be compared to an opponent trying to block a shot in a basketball game. The opposing player will often stick his body, face, or hands in the offensive player's face so that the offensive player will become disoriented, blocked, and unable to advance.

Satan doesn't want you or me to send the ball through the net for two points, so to discourage this, he brings his battle—your stronghold—as close to you as possible. Often, that means your battle is being waged within you—within your mind, will, emotions, and body.

When the battle is that close, you need a powerful weapon to turn the tables on the Enemy. We reach for the sword. But let's make sure we understand that this sword doesn't belong to you.

Pray today for strength to withstand the up-close, personal assaults of the Enemy that are bound to come your way.

Paul makes it clear in Ephesians 6:17; this is not your sword. It's not the church's sword. It's not the sword of good works or even religion. It's not the preacher's sword. This is the sword of the Spirit. In fact, it is the only tool we are told that the Spirit uses in the spiritual realm.

> If the sword belongs to the Spirit, why are we instructed to take it up?
> How can we take up something that belongs to someone else?

It is the Spirit who uses this sword in the heavenly places to deliver a deathblow to our Enemy. Because that's true, you need to remember that you cannot deliver that deathblow yourself. If you try, you will soon discover that God instructed you in how to use the sword of the Spirit for a very good reason.

> Read about Peter's experience with a physical sword in John 18:1-11.
> How did Jesus respond to Peter's actions?

> What was wrong with what Peter was trying to do?

Peter made the same mistake Moses did in the Old Testament. He saw his people languishing in slavery and took it upon himself to become their deliverer. In the process, he killed an Egyptian taskmaster. Similarly, Peter saw it as his job to deliver

Jesus by cutting off the ear of one of the men who had come to arrest Him. Both learned that the authority for victory in the spiritual realm is rooted and grounded in God, not in us. Jesus rebuked Peter to let him know that his human approach was not needed for this battle. The same holds true for you and me.

> What are some earthly resources you have turned to for help in your battle against strongholds?

> Does that mean there is no place for such resources? How might things like counseling, support groups, and books be appropriately used in the spiritual battle?

One reason so many of us lose our battles is that we have turned primarily to earthly resources, methods, and views to try and do battle against someone who is not human. There is great value in some of these methods, but we must first and foremost recognize the spiritual nature of all our struggles. When we do, we'll see that real victory can be secured only in the spiritual realm. All of the human resources might help with the aftereffects and casualties of the battle, but they can't take the place of what God has given us to wage war.

Paul didn't say, "Take up your sword"; he said to take up the "sword of the Spirit." Your best methods and intentions can't compete with an Enemy who is fighting in a different capacity than you or I could ever function. The only way to defeat this Enemy and walk in victory is to do so according to prescribed means. When you choose to utilize a human method to go up against a spiritually derived battle, you nullify God's power in your fight.

> Read Romans 12:19. What do you think it means to "leave room" for God's wrath?

When we are wronged, the most natural thing to do is get revenge. But when we do that, in our own power and according to our own desires, we fail to "leave room" for the wrath of God.

How does that principle apply more broadly to the way we wage war in the spiritual realm?

"Leaving room" means letting go of your approach to spiritual battles and letting go of your need to respond to your emotions. God doesn't sanction our approach, and our emotions are unreliable. Therefore, we must take God's approach by aligning our emotions underneath His authority and putting on His full armor. We trust in His methodology and timing, believing the battle belongs to Him. Because it does, we must not take matters into our own hands. We submit ourselves to His methodology. When we do that, we pick up the Spirit's sword rather than our own.

What is one stronghold in your life that you have tried to fix on your own? How does your approach to that stronghold need to change in order to submit to God's methodology and His choice of weapon?

In order to see the Enemy sliced and diced as he ought to be, we have to believe in the power of the dagger. There is so much power in the sword of the Spirit that God gave it to us as the only weapon to be used offensively. Maybe this sword is the only offensive piece in the collection because it's the only one we need.

Pray today that you will apply God's prescribed method to the battles in your life.

# DAY 3     WORD

Paul wants us to know the exact composition of this offensive weapon. The sword of the Spirit is the Word of God.

Why do you think this dagger like weapon is linked to the Word of God?

On the scale below, rate your knowledge of the Word of God

Not familiar        Somewhat familiar        Very familiar

What ways are you actively pursuing a greater love and knowledge of God's Word?

In order to fully comprehend what is being referred to as the Word of God, we need to consider the different Greek terms used.

Read 2 Timothy 3:16 and 2 Peter 1:20. What does the "Word of God" refer to in these passages?

When Scripture uses the Greek word *graphe* to refer to the Word of God, it's referring to the writings of God, or the Bible. When you attend church and the preacher says to turn in your Bible to a certain passage, you are holding the graphe in your hands—the 66 books, that compose the canon of Scripture.

If someone asked you what the Bible is, how would you respond? Why?

What is the right way to use the Bible? Why did God give it to us?

Some people look to their Bibles the same way others look to a rabbit's foot, assuming that it alone brings about the power needed to live a life of victory in a fallen world. But to place your Bible in your car thinking it will somehow stop an accident from happening or buying an oversized Bible and putting it on your coffee table, thinking it will ward off anything negative and evil, is just a form of magic.

The Bible was never meant to be a talisman; it was meant to be read, loved, and memorized. The Bible is the primary means God has given us to know Him; it is the written revelation of Himself and His plan for the universe. It shapes, then, the basis on which we view all of reality.

But Paul did not use the word *graphe* for the Word of God in Ephesians 6.

Is that surprising to you? Why or why not?

Does that mean the Bible plays no role in spiritual warfare? Think back
and record a summary of its importance in the battle.

Another Greek term for the Word of God found in Scripture is the word *logos*.
Logos refers to the message of the book or the meaning of the words. When you
read your Bible, attend a Bible study, or hear a sermon that explains the meaning of
the text being referenced, you are experiencing and interacting with the logos. You
started with the graphe and have progressed into the logos.

Read John 1:1. What does the word *Logos* refer to in this passage?

What does that indicate about Jesus' identity?

Jesus is called the Logos in this passage because He was sent as God's messenger—
to present God to human beings and embody His message to us. The graphe is the
message written, while the logos is the message given. Logos is the understanding
of the written record of stories, events, and letters that we come into contact with
in the Bible.

Read another reference to logos in Hebrews 4:12. List below the
attributes of the word from this passage.

How is this different from the graphe?

The logos is more than just words on paper. The logos is alive and active. It is a force with energy behind it to accomplish a specific goal. To accomplish that goal, the logos is sharp and piercing, dividing your soul from the new spirit God has placed within you.

Jesus embodies these characteristics. Time and time again, we see that he was able to look deep into the hearts of people and judge and discern what was at their core. Likewise, when we allow the logos of God to penetrate and take deep root within us and as we meditate on how to fully understand God's truth, it will reveal our hearts to such a degree that we will be able to discern right from wrong and truth from lie. It will penetrate us deeply, creating a powerful impact.

How often do you feel the impact of the logos in your own life?

What might need to change in your habits and approach to Bible study in order to feel it more frequently?

Surprisingly, however, Paul doesn't use the word *logos* either in Ephesians 6. He chose a third word.

Pray that God will bring you into a deeper love of, appreciation for, and submission to all His Word.

# DAY 4    RHEMA

When Paul tells us to take up the sword of the Spirit, which is the Word of God, he's not talking about the graphe, the written Word of God. Neither is he talking about the logos. The logos, in Hebrews 4, was compared to a sword in its ability to penetrate within each person, but it's not this sword Paul had in mind. In Ephesians he used the Greek term *rhema*.

Rhema simply means *utterance, spoken word,* or *what has been declared.* But in this term we actually see these previous two words for sword coming together. Graphe is the written Word. Logos is the message of the written Word. Rhema is the specific declaration concerning the message of the written Word.

In your own words, how are those three terms related to one another?

Could you have the rhema without the other two? Why or why not?

What does that indicate about the nature of the rhema?

A person could own a Bible factory and publish thousands of Bibles every day and never have the power of the sword. A person could have great understanding of the message in the Scriptures but still not utilize the power of the sword against the Enemy. It's not until we read the written Word, understand its message, and *specifically apply that message to a given situation* that we begin to utilize the rhema.

So many Christians live defeated lives because they have not graduated from graphe to logos to rhema.

If a person is stuck on graphe, what is their relationship to the Bible like? Why doesn't that lead to victory?

What about logos? What is the life of a person stuck on logos like?

Why does moving through this progression lead to an offensive weapon like rhema?

Bringing your Bible to church isn't the same thing as using the sword of the Spirit. You've got the graphe in your hand, but you're not reading it and hearing God's Spirit teach you through it.

It's equally easy to get stuck in "logos land." You can try to understand the sermon, attend the Bible studies, and take notes on what you've learned without ever using that knowledge to battle the Enemy. Those things might penetrate deep inside you, but in close-up battle with the Enemy, on the evil day, you need the utterance of

God for your situation. You need to hear God speak—not in a general sense—but speaking to *you* and take that truth straight into the heart of Satan and his demons.

Have you ever read a certain passage in the Bible so many times through the years that you feel you know it by heart? And then one day, as you turn to that passage, thinking you already know everything in it, it's as if God takes a yellow highlighter and focuses your eyes on one verse, word, principle, or truth. Suddenly that familiar passage is speaking directly to the situation you are facing.

That is a rhema word—God speaking to you through the utterance of His word.

Has that ever happened to you? Describe the instance below, along with the specific verse of Scripture.

God's spoken word was powerful enough to completely change things in the very beginning. He's able to bring things into existence out of nothing. We read in Genesis 1:3, "God said, 'Let there be light,' and there was light.' " Repeatedly at the beginning of Genesis, we read that God said something was so, and it came to be so. All God had to do was speak the word, and whatever he spoke came about.

In other words, the spoken word (rhema) had the power within it to do whatever the spoken word said to do. The rhema was the Spirit's dagger that God used to bring things into being.

That's why it's so important to study, learn, and engage in God's Word. When we do, we will begin to see that God still has the power to simply speak and dispel darkness.

And if we understand this, we must also know that Satan understands its power as well. Since God's Word is so powerful, Satan knows all he has to do is twist God's Word, and it will become a dull sword, unable to carry out its purpose both as an internal sword (logos) and as an offensive weapon (rhema).

As you pray today, express your confidence in God's Word to bring about whatever He desires.

## DAY 5

# TAKING UP THE SWORD

Satan has been dulling the sword of God's Word from the very beginning. In fact, he often uses the same tactic with us that he did with Adam and Eve. It all centers on the Word of God.

Read Genesis 3:1-7. How was Satan's deceptive tactic related to the word of God?

Have you ever succumbed to a similar temptation? One that had its root in questioning the word and promises of God?

"Did God really say?" Satan led with this question because he knew if he could mix up God's directions in Eve's mind, he would reduce its power to defeat him.

In fact, Satan loves it when you say things like, "Well, I think … " or "My opinion is …" or "My friends say … " He loves it because responses like that show we are trusting in our own ability to define reality instead of standing under the authority of God. Satan knows there is no power in what you, your family, or your friends think or feel. He'll leave you alone to collect that type of information through TV talk shows, self-help books, or phone calls to your family and friends. He's not scared of that at all.

But as soon as you start saying, "Well, God says … " and jabbing those words directly into his midsection, he starts running. Satan is unable to stand against the powerful force of the utterance of God. But don't take my word for it. Jesus gives us the perfect example of how to take up the sword of the Spirit, which is the Word of God.

Read Matthew 4:1-11. How did Jesus get into the wilderness? Does that bother you? Why or why not?

What similarities can you find between this story and the story in Genesis 3?

What is the difference between the way Jesus and Eve responded to temptation?

It's interesting to note that the Spirit led Jesus straight into the face of the Devil. It's crucial to recognize this because we see in the later verses that Jesus used the rhema (utterance of God) to defeat the Devil. God went on the advance against Satan by leading Jesus to him, and Jesus responded by using the offensive tool, the sword of the Spirit, to overcome him.

Jesus, after fasting for 40 days, was understandably hungry. Satan saw this as an opportune time to strike, sensing that Jesus was at His weakest. So he attacked at a perceived vulnerable point and tried to capitalize on Christ's legitimate need for food.

Have you seen the same thing happen in your life? What is one example of Satan's corrupting a legitimate need or desire in your mind and tempting you to satisfy it in an illegitimate way?

How would you have responded in that instance if you followed
the example of Jesus?

What Jesus didn't do in this situation is just as important as what He did. By saying, "It is written" (vv. 4,6-7), and then using the full force of the Word of God, Jesus did not enter a long debate or dialogue with Satan about the subject. He simply said, "It is written" and shut the Enemy down.

Quick stab with the dagger.

What kinds of practices must have been a regular part of Jesus' life
in order to respond like this?

If the living Word, Jesus, needed to use the rhema word to deal with the Enemy, then how much more must we need to rely on the same weapon? Jesus embodied perfection in His thoughts and reasoning, but He still didn't approach Satan on His own. He overcame Satan with the Word of God. Satan tried two more times, but after three thrusts of the dagger, he couldn't handle any more and left as quickly as he had come. Maybe you are wondering why the same doesn't happen for you. Satan won't leave you alone. He comes back again and again. My question for you is whether you are using the Word of God to make him leave you alone.

If you want victory, you've got to read, study, and memorize the graphe. You've got to dwell on it to discern the logos. And then you've got to actually deliver the blow with the rhema. When you do that, you've taken up the sword, and, as James says, you can "resist the Devil, and he will flee from you" (Jas. 4:7).

Pray today that you will recall specific passages of Scripture that will
enable you to go on the offensive in the spiritual battle.

---

1. Harold Hoehner, *Ephesians: An Exegetical Commentary* (Grand Rapids, MI: Baker Academic, 2002), 581.
2. John Stott, *The Message of Ephesians* (Downer's Grove, IL: Intervarsity Press, 1979), 282.

THE FULL ARMOR
IN REAL LIFE

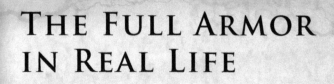

## SESSION 8

# THE FULL ARMOR IN REAL LIFE

## GETTING STARTED

1. Share one insight you gained through your personal devotions this week.

2. Do you think, after this week, you appropriately prioritize the reading, study, and memorization of God's Word?

3. What is one significant way you have seen your life change over the course of this study?

## ARMING UP

**Watch the teaching segment from the DVD using the viewer guide below.**

_____ is how you put on and wear the armor of God.

Prayer is _____ permission for _____ interference.

God has organized the world to work through _____.

There are many things God does not intervene in unless _____ to do so.

Prayer is the _____ means of entering into the supernatural realm in order to utilize the armor.

The best way to pray is to throw God's _____ back at Him.

Prayer is not making God do something; it is _____ by faith what He has already planned to do.

*kairos*—an _____ time

Paul is calling for _____ and _____ prayer
for God to intervene in your circumstances.

To pray in the _____ is to mouth words with no spiritual attachment
to them.

To pray in the _____ is to bring spiritual truth into your conversation with God.

Daniel found out what God had to _____, he prayed, and then was
granted _____.

Warfare in the spiritual realm results in _____ in receiving God's
answers to prayer.

Don't keep praying to get God to answer; you keep praying for God
to intervene and keep Satan from _____ the answer.

God answers when you ask based on His _____.

It's _____ _____ if the Enemy is trying to distract your prayer.

**Discuss the teaching with your group, using the questions below.**

1. What is one thing you wish you could change about your prayer life?

2. What role does prayer play in seeing victory in spiritual warfare?

3. Share with your group one specific way they might pray for you as your
   study together ends.

**Close with prayer.**

Video sessions available at www.bhpublishinggroup.com/victoryinspiritualwarfare
or with a subscription to smallgroup.com

# GET IN THE FIGHT!

**Scripture Memory:**

"Pray at all times in the Spirit with every prayer and request, and stay alert in this with all perseverance and intercession for all the saints." Ephesians 6:18

▮ Share with someone who was not a part of this study a few things God has taught you in regard to spiritual warfare.

▮ Consider leading another Bible study group through *Victory in Spiritual Warfare*.

# SESSION EIGHT

A world-champion bodybuilder went to Africa on a tour to promote good health and physical fitness. One day he held a fitness-awareness seminar in a small, remote village. He had just finished demonstrating all of the different ways he could cause his muscles to bulge and contract all over his body when the local tribal chief stopped him.

"What you have shown is impressive. But what do you use those muscles for?" The bodybuilder answered, "Bodybuilding is my profession. This is my job."

The chief followed with another question: "You don't use those muscles for anything else?" The bodybuilder shook his head, "No."

"What a waste," said the chief. "What a waste to have all those muscles and not use them."

The same could be said for any believer who has access to the full armor of God but does not use it to walk in victory. In this final session I want to identify five prominent strongholds that often keep people in bondage.

A *stronghold* can be defined as *that which results from something invisible in the spiritual realm cooperating with something visible in the physical realm that keeps a person trapped in an addiction or a negative life pattern.* Overcoming a stronghold always involves a spiritual solution because strongholds are rooted in spiritual causes.

For each of the following strongholds, I've included an explanation of the stronghold, God's viewpoint on the stronghold, and the solution to the stronghold.

*Ready for victory? Let's get practical.*

# DAY 1

# CHEMICAL STRONGHOLDS

Popeye the Sailor Man was constantly brutalized in cartoons and comic books by an overgrown bully named Bluto. He regularly sought to wreak havoc on Popeye in a number of ways. But every time it looked as if Popeye could not go one minute longer, he reached for a can of spinach. After popping open the can and downing its contents, a new Popeye emerged—strong and victorious.

Many of us today have developed Popeye syndrome. When life's circumstances or the people around us bring us pain and anguish, causing us to feel beaten down, burdened, lonely, or stressed, we reach for a can. Or a bottle. Or a cigarette. Or any other chemical in order to provide a quick fix of relief to a long-term problem.

What's your chemical of choice to turn to for relief during times of stress or pain? Alcohol? Nicotine? Caffeine?

When are some specific times when you feel as though you simply must have that chemical?

What might those times indicate about the manner in which you are using the chemical?

*Chemical stronghold* can be defined as *a dependency on chemicals to address, escape, cope with, or be relieved from the struggles and stresses of life.* People with chemical strongholds often reveal themselves through statements like "I just need a drink to unwind" or "I just need a smoke to reduce the stress" or even "I'm ugly until I get my first cup of coffee." All three have really said the same thing: "I can't be what I was meant to be without the presence of these chemicals."

Do you ever make statements like that in order to justify your dependence on a substance? When?

Is there really anything wrong with that? What's the big deal?

How do you think God would respond to statements like that?

Sure, coffee doesn't have the same consequences as cocaine, but they're similar in this: we convince ourselves that we need them, and in so doing, we become mastered by them.

Read Romans 6:12-14. According to this passage, what are we unable to do when we are mastered by something?

We are meant to offer all of our bodies as instruments of righteousness to God for His purposes. But we can't do that if we are slaves to substances. According to Paul, though, we have been made alive in Christ by grace, and that life now has the ability to dominate our responses.

In other words, the key to overcoming chemical strongholds is to know who you are.

When a believer in Christ loses sight of who God has made them to be in Christ, they will turn to cheap substitutes. They miss that God has already given them everything they need for godliness, along with every spiritual blessing in the heavenlies. We must remember, in the case of chemical strongholds, that God has given us everything we need in Christ to cope and deal with any stress, pain, or disappointment.

We must claim that promise by faith and then throw it in the face of the Enemy when he tries to convince us that we *need* something else besides Jesus. We must turn to the Spirit, not the bottle, when life comes crashing in on us.

> Read Ephesians 5:18-20. Why do you think being filled with the Spirit is compared to being drunk in this passage? How are they similar? How are they different?

Be filled with the Spirit and let Him satisfy what you need. But being filled with something involves having more than a desire for it. It is an ongoing action. Just as a person who depends on alcohol to get them through the day will have a drink in the morning, one at lunch, one in the afternoon, and so on, we must have an ongoing filling of the Spirit.

> Look back at verses 19-20. How is that filling of the Spirit maintained?

Simply stated, the Holy Spirit's presence involves worship—and not just showing up at church on Sundays; being filled with the Spirit means making worship a lifestyle. When you do that, you'll find that your cravings begin to change. Rather than living as a slave to what you crave, you are free to be all you were created to be.

Remember, that's how God created you in Christ—not to be dependent on substances for comfort but to be filled with the Spirit.

> Pray today about the specific situations that lead you to believe you need a substance to bring relief. Commit instead to God's truth—that you have been made alive in Christ and now have the ability to offer your body as an instrument of righteousness.

# SEXUAL STRONGHOLDS

We have all been affected, in some form or another, by the increase in sexual awareness in our culture. Things that would have shocked moviegoers 15 or 20 years ago now regularly show up on TV. Magazines routinely display images of scantily clad models or celebrities posed in sexually alluring positions. The Internet has delivered pornography, in every conceivable form, not only to the home but often to phones as well.

> Specifically, how has the increase in sexual awareness affected you and your family?

What makes a sexual stronghold more difficult to overcome is its secretive nature. A person can have a sexual stronghold and never have sex. But that person can be addicted to pornography, fantasizing, or achieving personal gratification while using an illegitimate means to do so. People who would never go and do anything sexually wrong often find as much satisfaction by thought as they would by action.

> Read Romans 1:18-27. Look at the verb tenses here. When is the wrath of God being revealed?

> Was the root sin in this passage sexual? If not, what led to the sexual impropriety?

The devolution of man's sexuality is directly tied to idolatry. The stronghold of sex on any level is not first and foremost a problem with sex. After all, God designed each of us with a natural, healthy desire for sex. Sex, within the confines of marriage, is one of the greatest pleasures we are able to experience on earth. But when we refuse God's legitimate means of satisfying that desire, we show that we have exchanged the truth of God for a lie. In so doing, we have become idolaters.

God created sex. The Bible tells us that all God created was good. So the issue is not whether sex is good or bad; the issue is whether sex is being used according to God's intentions and within His boundaries.

> What are some of the good purposes for which God created sex?
> List them below.

The purpose of sex was both to inaugurate a covenant and to renew it. The act of sex, in terms of God's covenantal purposes, was so critical that He attached blood to it. Blood is often attached to covenantal or sacrificial actions in order to signify the seriousness of the covenant. Think about the rite of circumcision for the males in Israel or even the shedding of Jesus' blood on the cross. When a man marries a virgin, there is blood on their honeymoon night as the hymen has been designed to break and produce the shedding of blood.

> Do you honestly think of sex in those serious terms? If not, what has led
> to that lack of seriousness?

There are numerous places in Scripture that remind us of the significance of sex to God.

Read 1 Thessalonians 4:3-5 and 1 Corinthians 6:19-20. What principles regarding sex do you find in these passages?

Paul directly ties sexual morality with sanctification and knowing God. Then he takes it a step further in 1 Corinthians, saying we have been purchased through the death of His Son and therefore are to use our bodies to bring Him glory.

But how do you do that? It's going to take more than a cold shower. The main step in overcoming a sexual stronghold is recognizing your identity in Christ.

Read 1 Corinthians 6:9-13. Would you say this passage is good news or bad news? Why?

Paul wrote this to the church at Corinth, which had every manner of scandal and sexual activity going on in it. But he tells them, "Such *were* some of you." He is saying that as a believer in Jesus Christ, you are no longer a homosexual. You are no longer an adulterer. You are no longer a fornicator. You are a saint who views pornography. You are a saint committing a sexual indiscretion.

Do you see it? We must return to who we have been made to be in Christ and align our thinking and behavior accordingly.

If God has enough power to raise Jesus Christ from the dead, friend, He has enough power to give you the strength to resist and flee from sexual temptation. The solution is found by turning to Him, replacing your thoughts with His thoughts on who you are in Christ, and trusting Him to deliver you.

If you are caught in a pattern of sexual sin, be encouraged as you pray today. Trust in God's power to deliver you as you renew your mind with these truths.

# DAY 3

# EATING STRONGHOLDS

One of the most overlooked strongholds in America today is that of eating. In Christian circles we frequently condemn the alcoholic, the drug addict, or the porn addict, all while excusing the food addict.

Do you see eating as a stronghold that needs to be conquered? Why or why not?

Think about it more broadly. Does this stronghold show up only in overeating? How else might it manifest?

An eating stronghold might show up in eating too much but also might appear in eating too little or eating too much, only to purge later. An eating stronghold exists when food, the presence of or the lack of, becomes the dominant factor in someone's life. A dependence on food can offer a way to escape, to feel in control, to gain comfort, or even to inflict self-punishment.

Although the object of eating strongholds is food, the cause of them is not. Food is merely the symptom.

Read 1 Corinthians 10:1-7. Then read the psalmist's words in Psalm 78:19-31. In what sense were the people idolaters? What were they worshiping?

Compare these passages to Philippians 3:18-19. Where do you find similarities?

Your god or your idol is whatever you obey. If food calls to you, as it did to some of the Old Testament Israelites, and you obey it outside God's will for its use in your body, you have made food an idol. Food must be brought into its proper perspective within the purposes and program of God.

List some of the correct purposes and uses of food below. Then read 1 Corinthians 10:31.

You and I must desire and must be willing to glorify God in our eating. We were, in fact, uniquely created to bring glory to God through our lives. God paid top dollar for us in the form of His precious Son; He wants us to treat our bodies in a way that reflects His value of us. When you view and value your body as a tool for reflecting God's glory, it becomes difficult to surrender it to anything that might bring it damage.

After recognizing this, we must begin to move from self-disciple to Spirit discipline. One of the clearest ways to see the difference in these things is through something most of us are familiar with: dieting. The problem with most diets is that they are usually tied to willpower. That's fine, except for the fact that the human will is limited.

You may want to stop yourself from eating or make yourself start eating, for that matter, but at some point you will run out of will.

Can you recall a specific instance like that with food?

We need a power beyond our own, which is what the Holy Spirit supplies to us. When the Holy Spirit's power is supplied through grace, He aligns your thinking under the viewpoint of God that says your body is here to glorify God. Food then becomes a means to the end of doing that.

Read 1 Timothy 4:1-5. What do you think the word *sanctified* means?

In what sense might we apply that word to food?

*Sanctified* means that something is *set apart for a special purpose.* Sanctification turns mealtime into spiritual time. By receiving your food in a spirit of thanksgiving and with a desire to bring Him glory in your body, you change the way you approach food. Now instead of eating to satisfy your flesh, emotions, or desires, you are eating to satisfy God's destiny in you.

When you pray, say, "Lord, I thank You for this food and also for my body You have given to me. I don't want to dishonor You by what I put in it. I want to bring You as much glory as I can. So will you have the Holy Spirit convict and let me know when I have gone too far with this food or when I have turned to food to meet a spiritual need when You want me to meet You?"

Pray the previous prayer or one similar to it this week when you eat.

# DAY 4 | EMOTIONAL STRONGHOLDS

Many Christians are held hostage by emotional strongholds like depression, anger, discouragement, frustration, inferiority complexes, fear, and countless other volatile feelings. People who are in emotional strongholds usually know it. When they wake up in the morning, they don't say, "Good morning, Lord." Rather, they say, "Good lord, it's morning." They struggle simply to survive, often living in a perpetual state of hopelessness, worry, or despair.

Does the previous description sound familiar? Are you now or have you ever been caught in an emotional stronghold?

How can you tell the difference between an emotional stronghold and just having a bad day?

Emotional strongholds dictate and even dominate your thoughts, choices, and quality of life. God never ordained for you to wake up every day depressed or paralyzed by fear. He didn't create you to carry anger around for 5, 15, or 50 years. Jesus didn't die for that. He died for the abundant life He promised to give (see John 10:10).

How do you think most people deal with emotional strongholds? List some of the ways below.

Rather than seeking to suppress emotional strongholds through distractions, medications, or entertainment, God wants to reveal the root behind what you are experiencing. Certainly, some emotional strongholds are tied to a physical cause, like a chemical imbalance. Those need to be addressed physically.

But many emotional strongholds are not physiological in nature. They are rooted in sin—either your sin or someone else's sin that has affected you. Maybe you were abused as a child, betrayed in a relationship, or abandoned. It wasn't your sin that created the stronghold of fear, insecurity, guilt, or shame, but it was still sin that caused it.

Trace back to the root of your emotional stronghold. What do you find at the cause?

How is that cause an example of sin?

There are three general categories of emotional strongholds. The first category includes strongholds rooted in the past. Emotional damage has been caused during a person's developmental years, either through trauma, neglect, or other negative factors. These situations create emotional grooves in our minds that eventually become adopted as the normal mode of thinking and perceiving.

Consider the story of Joseph in Genesis 37. What kind of emotional strongholds rooted in the past might Joseph have had to overcome?

The next categories of emotional strongholds are issues being dealt with in the present. Trials and tests you are currently facing attack your emotional well-being.

Consider Paul's trials recorded in 2 Corinthians 11:23-31. What kind of emotional strongholds from trials in the present might Paul have had to overcome?

The third category involves fear of the future. This is what we call worry. We worry when we are afraid about tomorrow.

Consider the story of Esther. What kind of emotional strongholds about the future might Esther have had to overcome?

Which of these categories do your emotional strongholds fit in?

The cure for any emotional stronghold does not come in denying that it exists. Just as you can't cure cancer by pretending you don't have it, you likewise can't overcome an emotional stronghold by wishing it weren't there. The key to overcoming emotional strongholds lies in understanding their root and addressing that thoroughly.

Friend, God saw what happened to you, what is happening to you, or what you are afraid might happen to you. Intimacy with Christ, which offers a perspective on God in all of His fullness, goodness, and power, is the key to overcoming emotional strongholds. When you know Christ in a real, abiding way and live according to His truth, whatever is going wrong in your life no longer has the final say.

Jeremiah lived this way. If anyone had a reason to be bound in an emotional mess, it would have been this prophet. His city was destroyed. His people were falling apart. His future looked bleak at best.

Read Jeremiah's response in Lamentations 3:19-24. What keeps you from responding to your stronghold the way Jeremiah did?

Hope can go a long way. Instead of dwelling on the circumstances, Jeremiah spoke hope into them. God can take a mess and make it a miracle if you put your hope in Him. I know your emotions may seem overwhelming, and you may even wonder how you could ever overcome them, but if you hope in God—replacing the lies holding you hostage with His truth—and address any related sin, He can turn emotional suffering into a victorious life.

Pray Lamentations 3:19-24 over your own situation today to express your hope in God.

# DAY 5

# FINANCIAL STRONGHOLDS

When the economy crashed some time ago, it revealed a certain level of financial irresponsibility that had caught up with us as a country. Beyond a national level, that kind of financial irresponsibility caught up with us as individuals as well. There is no more poignant way financial strongholds are being realized today than in the debt level of God's people.

Many in the body of Christ are living in economic slavery to the consumer debt that controls their lives. Americans are drowning in a sea of debt, and until we address the spiritual stronghold behind the financial reality, we will remain that way.

Most people end up enslaved to debt because they have believed certain lies about money and possessions. Can you think of any such lies that have led you into financial slavery?

Read Proverbs 22:7 and Psalm 37:21. Record below the improper and proper attitude toward money, according to these verses.

Read Luke 16:10-11. What, according to this passage, is the connection between financial and spiritual responsibility?

A refusal to handle money God's way can actually limit the responsibility God gives you regarding requests you might make for greater things. God's solution to the debt stronghold can be summarized with three simple words: *give, save,* and *spend.* Your financial freedom is inextricably tied to these three principles.

The first principle is the initial action that should happen any time you receive anything from God: give to God. The average Christian in America gives less than 3 percent of their income to God. Roughly 85 percent of Christians do not tithe, and approximately 40 percent of Christians give nothing at all. Essentially, mass larceny is taking place in the kingdom of God, and yet we still wonder why the kingdom is failing to advance in our nation and world.

> Read Malachi 3:8. Do you think of your giving this seriously? Why or why not?

> Read Matthew 6:19-24. Why is the way we spend our money an accurate gauge of what we love?

If you want to know what's utmost in your affections, just follow the money. That's what Jesus said. Our attitudes toward giving will accurately reveal two things: whether we trust God, and whether we believe God to be sovereign—that is, whether we acknowledge His ultimate ownership of all things.

God is your source. Everything else is just a resource. Never treat the resource like the source, because the resource will then control you.

> Read 2 Corinthians 8:9. What did Paul appeal to in order to motivate giving? Why is that an appropriate appeal to make?

The second word is *save*. An estimated 35 percent of all Americans have no savings. While debt is paying for yesterday, savings is putting away something for tomorrow.

Compare Proverbs 21:20 and Luke 12:16-21. How do we reconcile these passages with each other?

Given these passages, what is the right, God-honoring way to save?

Saving becomes idolatrous when you start to trust in your savings for your security and contentment instead of God. A good way to avoid this mistake is to remind yourself that one of the primary reasons you are saving is not so that you can have a comfortable life; it's so that you can give away more! In this way we can ensure we're still looking to God as our provider.

It's only after we look at these first two words that we can finally come to the third: *spend*. We have to spend money, but the question is whether we spend it well. If we don't manage our money, our money will manage us—our emotions, time, and decisions. To manage money well, we've got to have a spending plan. A budget. Without that plan we'll always spend more than we make.

But undergirding that plan is a stable confidence that God Himself is enough for us to be content.

Read how Paul expressed this sentiment in 1 Timothy 6:8-10. Did Paul say money itself is a root of evil? Why is that an important distinction to make?

When you align your finances underneath God's overarching principles of giving, saving, and spending, you will see God free you from the stronghold of debt.

Pray today for a proper attitude toward money. Repent, if necessary, of your greed and your improper use of finances.

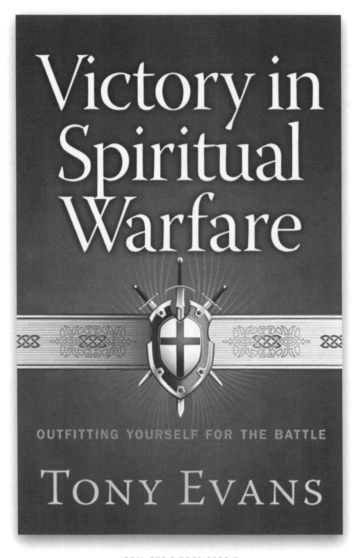

# Victory in Spiritual Warfare

OUTFITTING YOURSELF FOR THE BATTLE

## TONY EVANS

ISBN: 978-0-7369-3999-7

# Tony EVANS
## THE URBAN ALTERNATIVE

At The Urban Alternative, the national ministry of Dr. Tony Evans, we seek to restore hope and transform lives to reflect the values of the kingdom of God. Along with our community outreach initiative, leadership training and family and person growth emphasis, Dr. Evans continues to minister to people from the pulpit to the heart as the relevant expositor with the powerful voice. Lives are touched both locally and abroad through our daily radio broadcast, weekly television ministry and internet platform.

# PRESENTING AN
# ALTERNATIVE TO:

## COMMUNITY OUTREACH

Equipping leaders to engage public schools and communities with mentoring, family support services and a commitment to a brighter tomorrow.

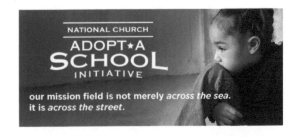

## LEADERSHIP TRAINING

Offering an exclusive opportunity for pastors and their wives to receive discipleship from Drs. Tony & Lois Evans and the TUA staff, along with networking opportunities, resources and encouragement.

## FAMILY AND PERSONAL GROWTH

Strengthening homes and deepening spiritual lives through helpful resources that promote hope and health for the glory of God.

TONYEVANS.ORG